The Roads of Fife

The Roads of Fife

OWEN SILVER

A Scottish History and Culture Paperback

JOHN DONALD PUBLISHERS LTD
EDINBURGH

ISBN O 85976 160 6

Exclusive distribution in the United States of America
and Canada by Humanities Press Inc.,
Atlantic Highlands, NJ 07716, USA.

The publisher acknowledges the financial assistance of
the Scottish Arts Council in the publication of this
volume.

Phototypeset by Newtext Composition Ltd., Glasgow
Printed in Great Britain by Bell & Bain Ltd.

Preface

Accounts of roads and their development in Britain have necessarily been confined, by the very breadth of the subject, to historical periods, to particular topics or to a selected region. An archaeological study of roads during the Roman occupation has covered the whole of Britain,[1] and roads over the same area have been included in several studies of the growth of communications.[2] While advances in the technology of road-building and of vehicle design have been amply described,[3] few direct references are made to Scotland, and the major works on the history of road administration are primarily concerned with England.[4]

One work comprising case studies of changing local road patterns up to the turnpike period includes some Scottish material,[5] but the only comprehensive accounts of turnpike growth refer almost entirely to England or Wales.[6] Among books pertaining to Scotland, the main interest has been in the eighteenth-century military roads in the Highlands[7] and their successors,[8] while in specialist journals may be found an introduction to the Scottish statute labour system[9] and a history of the roads of Kirkcudbright.[10] Individual roads and bridges have also been examined, from an archaeological viewpoint.[11]

This book sets out to survey the background to road improvement in the Scottish Lowlands, and to chart the development of the road system in Fife as an example of this process. It is hoped that it will serve as a general introduction to the local study of roads in Scotland, and that events in Fife might provide a basis for comparison.

References have been cut to a minimum, particularly where a source may easily be found from its year, or in the case of the statistical accounts, from its parish.[12] Precise references to the Acts of Parliament, to manuscript sources in Edinburgh and to the records of the various Fife road authorities may be found in the theses of Dr Stephen[13] and of the author,[14] copies of which are lodged in the public libraries of St Andrews, Kirkcaldy and Dunfermline.

For the less obvious locations, the six-figure grid references are given, the relevant Ordnance Survey sheets being Nos. 58, 59, 65 and 66. There is of course no substitute for the 1/25,000-scale sheets for detailed information, particularly in following the individual tracks mentioned in Chapter 12. All the older maps mentioned may be consulted in the National Library Map Room in Edinburgh,[15] but copies of Ainslie's map of 1775 can also be found at the Ceres Folk Museum and in St Andrews Public Library.

I am indebted to the many people who have helped me in acquiring material and for their courtesy in allowing me to quote from such sources. In particular, I would like to thank Mr A.G. Mackenzie, Librarian of St Andrews University, without whose consent it would have been impossible to assess the contents of the two hundred or more works written before 1840, relating to a study of Scottish roads. I am also grateful to Mr R.N. Smart and Mr G.D. Hargreaves for their guidance in the use of archive material, historical illustrations and maps; also to Mr John Tuckwell of the publishers for his great forbearance and a sure eye for tangled syntax; to Dr G.W. Whittington, without whose past guidance this would be quite unreadable; to Mr C.B. Bremner of the Department of Geography, who drew Figure 11.1 and gave invaluable help in the preparation of the other maps; to Mr P.G. Adamson of the University of St Andrews Photographic Unit, and finally to Dr P.H. Silver, who has stood in for the reader and encouraged the author to live dangerously.

Notes

1. Margary, I.D., *Roman Roads in Britain* London (3rd edn. 1973)

2. Appleton, J.H., *The Geography of Communications in Great Britain* London (1962); Dyos, H.J. and Aldcroft, D.H., *British Transport* Leicester (1969)

3. Copeland, J., *Roads and their Traffic 1750-1850* Newton Abbot (1968); Bird, A., *Roads and Vehicles* London (1969)

4. Jackman, W.T., *The Development of Transportation in Modern England* Cambridge (1916); Webb, S. and B., *English Local Government: The Story of the King's Highway* London (1920)

5. Taylor, C., *Roads and Tracks of Britain* London (1979)

6. Albert, W., *The Turnpike Road System in England 1663-1840* Cambridge (1962); Pawson, E., *Transport and Economy: The Turnpike Roads of Eighteenth Century Britain* London (1977). Treatment of Scottish roads is minimal.

7. Taylor, W., *The Military Roads of Scotland* Newton Abbot (1976)

8. Haldane, A.R.B., *New Ways through the Glens* London (1962)

9. Moir, D.G., 'The Roads of Scotland: 2: Statute Labour Roads', *Scottish Geographical Magazine (S.G.M.)* 73 (1), 73 (3) (1957)

10. Anderson, A.D., 'The Development of the Road System in the Stewartry of Kirkcudbright 1590-1890', *Transactions of the Dumfriesshire and Galloway Natural History and Antiquarian Society (T.D.G.N.H.A.S.)* 44 (1967)

11. Graham, A., 'Archaeology on a Great Post Road', *Proceedings of the Society of Antiquaries of Scotland (P.S.A.S.)*, 96 (1962-3). A study of the road from Berwick to Edinburgh. Curtis, G.R., 'Roads and Bridges in the Scottish Highlands: The Route between Dunkeld and Inverness 1725-1925', *P.S.A.S.* 110 (1978); Fenton, A. and Stell, G., *Loads and Roads in Scotland and Beyond: Road Transport over 6,000 Years* Edinburgh (1984)

12. All references to Fife parishes are to the facsimile edition of *The Statistical Account of Scotland*, 10, Grant, I.R. and Withrington, D.J. (eds.) Wakefield (1978) (referred to below as the *Old Statistical Account* or *OSA*) or to *The Statistical Account of Fifeshire* (contributed by the Ministers of the Respective Parishes) Edinburgh and London (1845) (referred to below as the *New Statistical Account* or *NSA*)

13. Stephen, W.M., The Industrial Archaeology of Fife 1790-1914 Unpublished Ph.D. thesis University of Strathclyde (1975)

14. Silver, O.B., The Development of the Fife Road System 1700-1850 Unpublished Ph.D. thesis University of St Andrews (1984)

15. Royal Scottish Geographical Society (Moir, D.G., ed.), *The Early Maps of Scotland to 1850*, 2, Edinburgh (3rd edn. 1983)

Contents

1
Creating and Keeping a Highway

The concept of a road as a deliberately built structure is relatively modern. Several thousand years ago, scattered communities roaming over a heavily wooded Fife needed to make repeated journeys between the best hunting grounds, according to the season. They also needed to find easy routes to obtain supplies of materials that did not lie readily to hand. A seasonal camp made by mesolithic hunters and fishermen was recently discovered at Morton, near Leuchars in Fife,[1] and among the remains were weapons and tools made from rock which could only be found in the Ochil and Sidlaw hills, over twenty miles away.

What relation did the tracks made by these early inhabitants have to those used by subsequent generations? Perhaps a clue is to be found in a study of the rapid transition from hunter to modern settlement in eighteenth-century Ontario,[2] where surveyors are found to have set out boundaries for new farmland and associated roads along well-worn trails formed by caribou and their Indian hunters. Many roads built for communication with adjacent settlements were superimposed on these ancient tracks and some of them form important elements of the modern transport network.

Admittedly, the change from trail to road was made in Ontario in as short a time as twenty years, whereas in Fife, even allowing for the Roman military roads to the west, the interval must be measured in millennia. By the time anything resembling a purpose-built road was attempted, the movement of deer had long been restricted, by woodland clearance and human settlement, to the pleasure grounds of the aristocracy. With the harsh game laws in force, the following of deer, particularly in the royal lands around Falkland Palace, would have been most unwise, however ancient the tracks.

Nevertheless, the Canadian example serves as a reminder that beneath the concrete and tarmacadam of many modern roads in Fife there would have been routes found convenient for beast and man, perpetuated by centuries of human passage. Some of the most rewarding tracks to be explored today are those which the modern road system has abandoned, and which furthermore express the needs of countless generations of travellers, on foot and on horseback rather than on wheels. Although built roads are a recent phenomenon, measures were already being taken in mediaeval times to ease the difficulties of travel and to protect the natural surface of the ground from the effects of traffic. Action might be limited to throwing stones or brushwood into soft places, or a more determined effort might be made to raise the road level by means of a causeway. This is what may have been referred to in 1506, when James IV paid five shillings to 'ane man biggit ane brig our ane moss'. Other causeways are mentioned in acts of parliament or of the privy council later in the century, sometimes referring to routes across boggy ground in open country, but more frequently to paved areas under heavy traffic through towns. One example is the Canongate of Edinburgh, where in 1593 a toll was authorised for its repair.

The word 'road', incidentally, does not seem to be found before the seventeenth century. Instead, the Scottish term 'gait' or the English 'way' was used. Where a particular route was acknowledged as of importance for the general public, it became a 'highway', and where it required the protection of the law it acquired the status of the 'King's Highway'.

The establishment and protection of a highway created problems wherever people threatened to intrude on the space it occupied. While a track connecting two families would be solely their concern, the means of access from a village to ground outside would require a restriction on the building of walls or houses by communal agreement. The greater the number of people affected, the more powerful the guarantor of free access had to be. Such protection had its benefits for the guarantor, since, as the Romans clearly knew, a ruler needed to ensure effective control over his dominions by keeping open the means of communication, if only for the movement of troops. Those to whom grants of land had been given in exchange for their support also needed to be watched to see they did not become unduly powerful. It helped if their lands could be scattered as widely as possible, a policy assisted in the course of time by the effects of marriage and inheritance. Plots could not so easily be hatched on the move.

An example of legislation intended to safeguard the mobility of the English monarch is to be found in 1285, when a statute required the clearing of a belt two hundred feet wide on either side of a highway, so that robbers would be deprived of cover. The King's Highway was at that time treated as a strip of land over which the right of unobstructed passage was reserved for the king and his subjects. In fourteenth-century Scotland it was an offence to encroach upon or obstruct a highway belonging to a superior, and this same preoccupation with keeping the way clear, rather than improving the condition of the surface, is still evident in later legislation. Thus in 1555 'all commoun hie gaittis' between towns and ports were to be 'observit and keipit'; it was also required 'that nane mak thame impediment or stop thairintill'.

An English act of parliament in the same year was far more specific, and spoke of 'amending of high waies, being now very noisom and tedious to travell in and daungerous to all passengers and caryages'. The act set out a system of compulsory parish labour service which was to be the basis for road repairs in England (and later in Scotland, as explained below) for over two hundred years.

It is not difficult to find reasons for the relative urgency of the English act. In both Scotland and England one of the biggest landowners had been the Church. Its abbeys and priories managed their estates efficiently and they, like other landowners, needed reliable communications. Many of the fine stone bridges that survive from the fifteenth century or earlier may be attributed to the various religious houses. For instance, we find that a bridge in Angus was built by the tenants of Coupar Abbey in 1473.[3] Dairsie Bridge, near Cupar, Fife, had probably been erected by Archbishop Spottiswoode of St Andrews in the late fourteenth century, and was restored by Archbishop James Beaton soon after 1521.[4] Once built, the upkeep of the more public bridges was, in the middle ages, regarded as a suitable object for acts of piety, a release from penance on this account having been recorded in 1394. However, by the mid-sixteenth century this source of wise administration and money was being lost through the break-up of the established church.

The effects on road and bridge maintenance were more severe in England than in Scotland, chiefly on account of the disparity between their population sizes and the differing extent of their respective commercial activities. In England the total population was over eight times greater, London being at least ten times bigger than Edinburgh and growing fast.

The supply of London, and a burgeoning export trade, brought much traffic onto English roads, whereas in Scotland at that time commercial development was almost static, only small quantities of surplus rural products, such as timber, wool and hides, being exported. Almost all the overland carriage was by means of pack animals, and long-distance haulage by wheeled vehicles was of negligible importance. Where heavy objects had to be moved across country it was common to use sledges, as may have been the case when blocks of stone from quarries near Strathkinness were taken for building work at Balmerino Abbey in the thirteenth century. The use of water transport for the latter part of the journey might well have been considered on reaching the River Eden, for this was the way heavy indivisible loads would normally travel.[5] Millstones, if indivisible, had the virtue of being their own wheels, and tenants were obliged to provide the motive power.[6] Their trundling from quarry to mill must have provided a lively spectacle.

The Royal Progress

Quite how far measures taken in Scotland were influenced by the legislative developments in England is not clear, but the accession of James VI to the English throne in 1603 provided the opportunity for a greater exchange of expertise in the administration of highways. English justices of the peace had been made responsible for bridges in 1531, and when justices came to be introduced into Scotland in 1610, they were instructed to be 'cairfull concerning the upholding and repairing of the briggis that are not utterly ruined, that some course may be taikin by the countery next adjacent to give some supplie for that matter'. They were also required by the privy council 'to provide for helping of the King's heich wayes . . . and speciallie to be careful that no privat person encroache on the same way', again emphasising their first duty: to keep the roads free from obstruction.

In 1616 the ability of central government to exercise control over the local road administrators was put to the test by the projected visit of the king to Scotland the following year. A more confident tone may be noted in the instructions issued by the privy council to the sheriffs, their deputes and the justices of the peace of each county along the route. Many of their requirements may be matched with the provisions of the English 1555 act, such as the attendance of workmen from the named parishes on 'so many days a week . . . as they shall be ordered'. Penalties for non-attendance were severe: those who would 'mak ony excuise, refuise, or delay upoun or under quhatsumevir cullour or pretext' were placed 'under the pane to be callit, persewit, and punist in their personis and goodis'.

Owners of land were expected to provide not only workers but also a range of tools. In the case of Linlithgowshire these were spades, shovels, picks, mattocks, crowbars ('gavellokis'), sledge hammers ('quarrell mellis'), iron wedges, hand barrows, wheel barrows, carts, sledges, horses and 'otheris workeloomes as they sall desyre to haif be the oversearis of the worke'.

It seems that a special effort was made to give the king a good impression at the beginning of his journey in Scotland, for just north of Berwick a section of road is described in some detail. A tenant on one side had dug it away and his neighbour opposite had 'biggit housis and yairdis foiranent the same'. The one standard decreed by the privy council was a minimum width which could be as much as twenty-one feet. A more usual width was sixteen feet and this was specified for that part of the route between Falkland and Perth which lay through the parishes of Auchtermuchty, Strathmiglo and Arngask, passing down the Glen of Abernethy. Although an account of the king's progress has been written,[7] we are not told whether the various parishes succeeded in providing a highway to this standard. Suspicions are aroused when one reads a report from the Marquis of Hamilton that between Lesmahagow and Drumlanrig, south of Glasgow, he could undertake to mend a way for horses, but not for coaches or carts.

The visit of 1617 presented a field day for the bureaucratic mind, not least of the problems being the transporting of the king's baggage. Lists were drawn up naming the constables in each parish, the number of ploughlands and the number of horses to be held in readiness. In Fife 2,329 horses could, in theory, have been mustered. After crossing the Forth on Monday 19th May, the baggage was to be carried to Falkland to be uplifted on the Wednesday morning for taking to 'the ferrie of Dundee'.

Such a concerted piece of organisation was not to be repeated for many years. It might be asked why a system of regular parish labour similar to that in England was not adopted at this stage. Several possible explanations present themselves. The slow pace of development for much of the seventeenth century, in what was a mainly rural economy, has already been noted. During the king's visit parliament had defined more closely the duties of the justices. Hopes may have persisted that they would now have been able to achieve with the necessary vigour the repairs needed to maintain roads to a tolerable standard. Once the need was accepted, the administrative machinery was there, its effectiveness limited only by the willingness of those in government or at county level to become involved. Thus, a dilapidated ford and causeway at the Gullets, where the River Leven emerged from

Loch Leven, was repaired only after a petition in 1621 to the privy council.

A proposal by King Charles I to emulate his father by visiting Scotland in 1628 expressed the wish 'that the high wayes may in lyke maner be made readie for our passage'. The privy council having given orders for the highways 'to be perfyte', subsequently claimed that the work had been done, but conveniently persuaded the king that there was no money for his expenses that year. The visit was put off till 1629, and again till the coronation in 1633. Although fresh instructions went out each time, there is no evidence that any work was ever done.

Strife and Recovery

The extension of the English civil war into Scotland and the involvement of religious interests created distinctly unfavourable conditions for progress in improving the roads. By 1650 the Scottish economy was in a desperate state; an expansion of cultivation evident in the 1620s and 1630s was abruptly checked. There were few ships left, trade had virtually ceased, and some towns were on the verge of starvation. Legislation in 1641 and 1655 strengthened the regulations and increased the penalties for obstructing highways, particularly those leading to harbours, which were to be 'maid patent to all his majesties leiges for carrieing and transporting of . . . victuall [and] fewalles . . .', thus underlining the need to keep townspeople supplied, particularly where much of the surrounding countryside had been devastated.

John Lamont of Newton, near Kennoway, records in his diary[8] the movements of Charles II in Fife after his coronation at Falkland in January 1651, and his departure before defeat at the Battle of Worcester in September. By 1653 the English forces were in possession of Falkland and were supplied with thirty-six loads of coal from Largo, while parishes in the East Neuk were required to carry coal to warm troops at Struthers.

The restoration of the monarchy to England in 1660 brought much-needed stability to Scotland, and marked the beginning of a period of slow improvement in the fortunes of agriculture and the growth of industries, including the export of coal and the manufacture of salt and textiles. Modest changes in rural estate organisation were being attempted which in the next hundred years were to alter the face of the Scottish lowland landscape.

Landowners who had travelled, particularly those returning from the Low Countries, were anxious to try out the new crops and methods of cultivation. The lessening of the rivalry between families and factions that had obliged them to live in fortress-like tower houses, such as Scotstarvit, with a following of armed retainers, brought the opportunity to acquire some of the luxuries which money, rather than power, could buy. Their thoughts turned to the ways they could maximise the income they could expect from their tenants.

These were commonly organised into ferme touns, several families combining together to work the scattered strips of land allotted to them in the infield from which their animals were normally excluded, and herding their animals in the outfield or common pasture beyond. Such a system produced only low yields and a bare subsistence livelihood, with little surplus left for rent in kind, still less in cash. In many cases they had little more to offer than their services to their laird, on his lands or in war.

These personal services became less and less important; indeed, a smaller number of tenants, with land reorganised into enclosed fields of the pattern now familiar to us, was in time to produce a dramatic increase in farm production, in tenants' incomes and in rents.

Roads fit for Wheels

The process was, however, slow and experimental at first. One of the key methods of improving fertility, under whatever system, was the application of lime. This had been recorded from the early seventeenth century on those lands within easy reach of limestone and of a supply of peat or coal. An improvement in roads would extend this practice considerably. The controlled grazing of livestock on the new crops of clover and turnips would require manageable parcels of land in uniform cultivation with the erection of barriers such as stone dykes and thorn hedges. Such changes could most easily be carried out by an enthusiastic landowner on ground he farmed himself, that is to say in the mains farm and parks around his residence. This is as far as the process of enclosure had gone in most areas by the end of the seventeenth century.

Even these tentative changes were beginning to affect locally the rights of the public to move freely over the landscape, choosing the best from amongst the band of multiple tracks that often constituted the highway. The landowner, for his part, could not shift the customary position of the highway without an appeal to a higher authority, as is illustrated by Scott of Scotstarvit's request in 1621 to divert the main road between the south coast of Fife and Cupar from one side of his residence to the other. In the latter half of the century the erection of enclosure dykes was becoming a common problem and an act was passed in 1661 giving power to divert any highway up to about two hundred yards without special permission.[9] Nineteen instances have been noted before the end of the century, of roads diverted under this act, of which at least one third referred to enclosures surrounding residences. A further act in 1669 required arable land adjacent to a highway to be enclosed by a ditch, dyke or hedge. One contemporary traveller was less than complimentary in describing some of the dykes he had seen, and commented, 'here and there they raise out of the road some little continued heaps of stone in the nature of a wall to secure their crops from the incursions of travellers'.[10]

Reforms in farm organisation could only proceed smoothly if tenants were given an interest in the future of their holdings through longer leases. They also benefited if they were free to dispose of their surplus crops at the nearest market and not have to take them, usually in wintertime, to their landlords' barns. Grain had traditionally been carried on packhorses, but it was now increasingly being carried over longer distances in carts, so that roads with firm surfaces would be needed if full loads were to be hauled, and if the roads themselves were not to be destroyed by such traffic.

To deal with the problem of road maintenance, something better than the spasmodic commandeering of local labour for specific occasions was called for. The answer for the majority of roads appeared to lie in a modification of the now well-tried English statute labour act of 1555. A comparison between the main provisions of the two acts is set out in Table 1.1

Late Seventeenth-Century Road Management

The preamble to the Scottish act of 1669 indicates that vague exhortations to justices were now considered insufficient to ensure the repair of roads. It begins, '. . . considering that the care of highways which hath been laid upon the justices of the peace hath yet for the most part proven ineffectual, in regard the saids justices have not had

Table 1.1
The Main Provisions of the English and Scottish Acts compared

	English Act of 1555	*Scottish Act of 1669*
The unit of road administration	The Parish	The County
The officers: Executive	Constable, Church wardens	Sheriff, Deputy, Justices of the Peace
To whom accountable	Justices of the Peace	Privy Council
Rewards for services	8d in the £ for collection of fines	Nil
Direction of road work	Surveyors	Justices and appointed overseers
Rewards for services	Unpaid (elected for one year only)	May pay wages to foremen
Labour service to be given	4 days (later increased to 6)	6 days
Persons liable for labour service	Householders, cottagers, labourers	Tenants, cottars and their servants
Persons exempt from service	Yearly hired servants	No exemptions
Provision of carriage, etc.	1 ploughland to provide 1 cart, 2 men	Persons liable to have horses, carts, sleds spades, shovels, picks, mattocks
Rate on land	Nil	Rate not more than 10s. in £100 valued rent

special orders and warrands for that effect . . .', and goes on to prescribe yearly meetings for the sheriff, depute and justices of each county.

The essential distinction between the two acts is the establishment of the county as the unit of road administration in Scotland, the sheriff and justices being accountable to the lords of the privy council. Responsibility in England had been placed a rank lower in the hierarchy of authority. The following year a modifying act enabled surveyors in Scotland who neglected their duties to be fined, labourers residing too far from the roads on which they were required to work could now make a monetary payment instead, and road work could not be enforced during the periods of seed time and harvest.

The burden of implementing the 1669 act, as amended, was too great for the sheriffs and justices alone, and by an act in 1686 they were to be joined in their duties by all the landowners of substance in each shire who were eligible to serve as commissioners of supply. The first function of the commissioners had been to raise local revenue for the king, but they now brought to their new task of managing the roads and bridges their experience of roads on their estates, their own prosperity being much dependent on the maintenance of good communications.

It is difficult to assess the performance of the gentlemen entrusted with the care of roads. Petitions for repair were usually couched in extravagant terms, but signs of a positive response are hard to find. Perhaps one indication of at least minimal adequacy could be the use of roads by wheeled transport, particularly passenger coaches. Thus, before the statute labour act, we find Archbishop Sharp in 1663 travelling by coach along the road from Kinghorn to Falkland, but for his other journeys in Fife that year only baggage and saddle horses are mentioned.[11] The same road was again to be used by Lady Rothes on her way to Edinburgh in 1696 for her two-horse coach.[12] It must be remembered, however, that although a twice-weekly conveyance carried mail from Edinburgh to Aberdeen in 1667,[13] only persons of rank and wealth could expect to travel by coach until well into the eighteenth century. The road north from Kinghorn was the most direct route between the ferry from Edinburgh and the ferry to Dundee. Accordingly, it would have had a high priority as a subject for repair.

Another, more hilly, road, from Kennoway to St Andrews was that on which Archbishop Sharp travelled on his last tragic journey in 1679. The route and his death on Magus Muir are graphically recorded,[14] and

Fig. 1.1. Murder of Archbishop Sharp in 1679. The bas-relief on the tomb in Holy Trinity Church, St Andrews was commissioned by his son within a few years of the event, and shows a carriage of the period drawn by six horses, as would be required for the steep pulls on the old road from Kennoway.

an illustration not long after the event depicts a coach of that period (Fig. 1.1.).

Although the 1686 road act required yearly joint meetings of justices and commissioners of supply to administer roads, this was seldom found convenient in practice. Delegation to meetings of one or the other body was common and a division of labour was adopted which varied from county to county. Since bridges could rarely be built without hiring masons, the task of repairing them usually fell to those in a position to raise the money — the commissioners of supply. This was certainly the case in the early eighteenth century in Forfarshire and Perthshire, but in Fife and Haddingtonshire the commissioners had charge of both roads and bridges, while in Lanarkshire the most active partners were the justices. Whatever the pattern of organisation, the repair of roads remained a daunting task, and it is hardly surprising to find few records of extensive work being carried out on roads until well into the eighteenth century.

The 1669 act had permitted the raising of a levy of up to six per cent on land values, but this was insufficient to pay for more than periodic repairs. Fortunately, the initial cost of a bridge would often be borne by a local landowner in his own interests, with the additional benefit of enhancing his prestige. A bridge could be seen by all as a desirable and necessary object for expenditure and it had the virtue of being finite. A

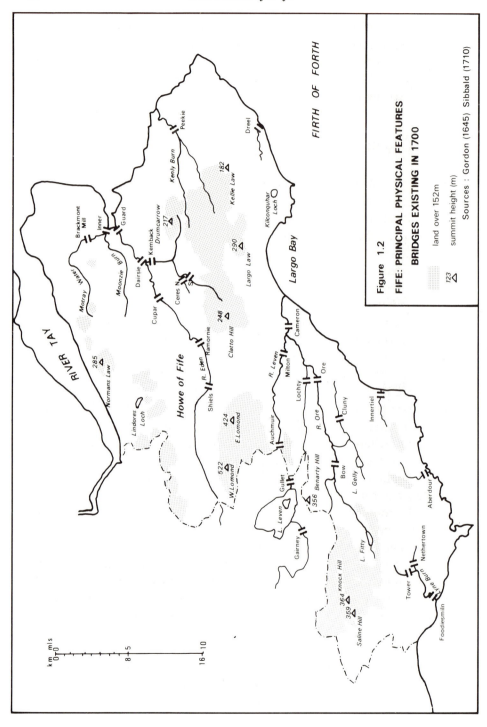

Figure 1.2

FIFE: PRINCIPAL PHYSICAL FEATURES
BRIDGES EXISTING IN 1700

Sources : Gordon (1645) Sibbald (1710)

road, on the other hand, though theoretically repairable by parish labour alone, represented in practice an extensive and bottomless pothole into which resources might be poured. The days when a landowner could hope to get credit with the local community for actually building a new road were yet to come.

Crossing the Fife Landscape

In Fife, most of the bridges to be found at the end of the seventeenth century had been shown on the map produced by James Gordon in 1645. Several are described by Robert Sibbald in a work begun in 1684,[15] and further bridges may be identified in ecclesiastical records. Figure 1.2 relates the bridges present in 1700 to the principal relief features of the county.

The upland areas have a predominantly west-east orientation. In the north, tilted slabs of hard volcanic rock show their upper edges along this axis and represent the remains of an arch joining them to the Sidlaws. In the overlying red sandstones the River Eden has excavated a broad valley between these northern lavas and the Lomonds. The latter form the highest feature in the peninsula and owe their prominence to the protection of a layer of hard dolerite, pierced by the two spectacular volcanic necks. Parallel ridges in the underlying pale sandstones extend into the East Neuk, while a similar pattern occurs to the south, where the River Leven is joined by its east-flowing tributaries to discharge into Largo Bay.

Many of the details of the landscape that have influenced the choice of traditional routes in Fife are part of the blanket cover of glacial material, through which the older rocks protrude only locally. Valley floors have been clogged by debris dumped by retreating ice sheets, and extensive bodies of water became marsh, necessitating detours and the use of hillside routes. Post-glacial meltwaters and a falling sea level have combined to produce, by rapid down-cutting, many steep-sided dens near the coast. Some of these presented problems for routes connecting coastal settlements. The burns were small by comparison with the Eden or the Leven, but could nevertheless create formidable obstacles in winter. A well-known tale in Fife is that of the 'stout gaberlunzie woman' who carried King James IV, disguised as a piper, across the Dreel Burn in Anstruther Wester, and was rewarded with his purse.[16] More alarming is the account by John Lamont in 1660 of a ford

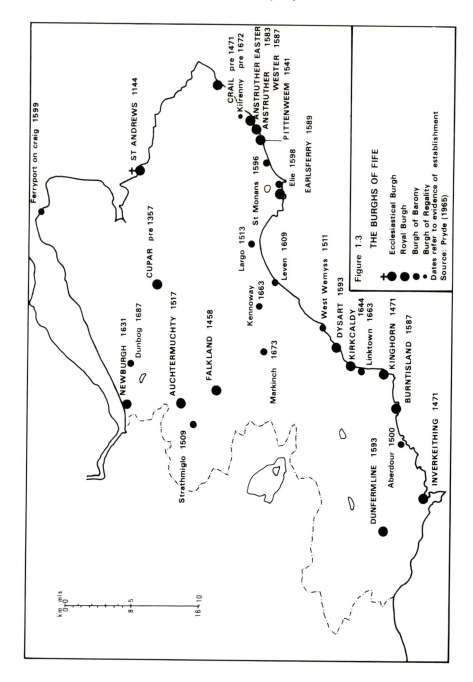

Ferryport on craig 1599

ST ANDREWS 1144

CRAIL pre 1471
Kilrenny pre 1672
ANSTRUTHER EASTER 1583
ANSTRUTHER 1587
WESTER 1541
PITTENWEEM 1587

CUPAR pre 1357

St Monans 1596
Elie 1598
EARLSFERRY 1589

Largo 1513
Leven 1609

NEWBURGH 1631
Dunbog 1687

AUCHTERMUCHTY 1517

FALKLAND 1458

Kennoway 1663

West Wemyss 1511
DYSART 1593

Markinch 1673

KIRKCALDY 1644
Linktown 1663
KINGHORN 1471
BURNTISLAND 1587

Strathmiglo 1509

DUNFERMLINE 1593
Aberdour 1500

INVERKEITHING 1471

Figure 1.3
THE BURGHS OF FIFE

+ Ecclesiastical Burgh
● Royal Burgh
● Burgh of Barony
• Burgh of Regality
Dates refer to evidence of establishment
Source: Pryde (1965)

km m/s
0
5
8
10
16

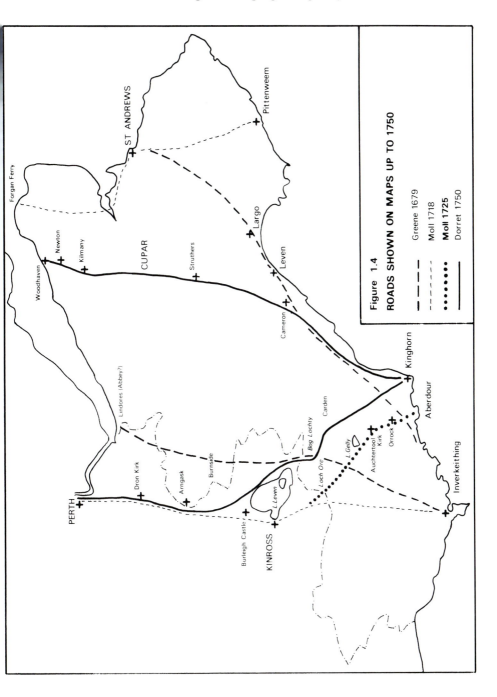

Figure 1.4

ROADS SHOWN ON MAPS UP TO 1750

Greene 1679
Moll 1718
Moll 1725
Dorret 1750

over the Kenly Burn, near Boarhills, where a woman was drowned after she and her husband attempted to cross in December on horseback.[17]

If we put together the positions of those bridges recorded up to 1700 and the distribution of settlements of sufficient importance as trading centres to have been granted burgh status[18] (Fig. 1.3), we can get a fair idea where road connections must have existed.

Thus, although little information is available regarding the administration of Fife roads before 1709, the year in which the records of the commissioners of supply begin, there is sufficient evidence to reconstruct a pattern of routes in use at that date. Some are confirmed by the few roads represented on the earlier maps (Fig. 1.4). Such lines as were shown are of dubious accuracy, but if to these we add the entries in the records relating to bridge and road repairs, we can anchor, piece by piece, the written data to what we can see on modern maps and, more importantly, on the ground.

NOTES

1. Taylor, C.C. *Roads and Tracks of Britain* London (1979), 8-9; Morrison, I.A., 'Prehistoric Scotland', in *An Historical Geography of Scotland*, Whittington, G. and Whyte, I.D. (eds.) London (1983), 10; Coles, J.M., 'Prehistoric Roads and Trackways in Britain', in Fenton, A. and Stell, G. (eds.), *Loads and Roads in Scotland and Beyond* Edinburgh (1984), 8

2. Burghardt, A.F., 'The Origin and Development of the Road Network of the Niagara Peninsula of Ontario', *Annals of the Association of American Geographers*, 59 (1969), 417-40; Coles (1984), 3

3. Rogers, C., *Rental Book of the Cistercian Abbey of Cupar-Angus* London (1879), 173

4. Ash, M., 'Dairsie and Archbishop Spottiswoode', in *Scottish Church History Society Records* 21 pt 2 (1976), 1

5. Smith, R.F., 'Quarry to Abbey: An Ancient Fife Route', *Proceedings of the Society of Antiquaries of Scotland (P.S.A.S.)* 83 (1948-9), 162-7

6. Whyte, I.D., *Agriculture and Society in Seventeenth Century Scotland* Edinburgh (1979), 32

7. Sinclair, G.A., 'The Scottish Progress of James VI', *Scottish Historical Review* 10 (1913), 21-8

8. Lamont, J., *The Chronicle of Fife, Diary of John Lamont of Newton 1649-72* Edinburgh (1810), 33

9. Whyte (1979), 101, 103

10. Morer, T., 'A Short Account of Scotland, 1689', in Brown, P.H. (ed.), *Early Travellers in Scotland* (1891), 266-90

11. Sharp, J., 'Journey Chairgis from Edinburgh to St Androis', in Brown (1891), 319-22

12. Bodie, W.G.R., 'Introduction to the Rothes Papers', *P.S.A.S.* 110 (1978-80), 406

13. Haldane, A.R.B., *Three Centuries of Scottish Posts* Edinburgh (1971), 17

14. Grierson, Dr., *St Andrews* Cupar (1838), 394

15. Sibbald, R., *The History, Ancient and Modern, of the Sheriffdoms of Fife and Kinross . . . a new edition* Adamson, L. (ed.) Cupar (1803) (originally published 1710)

16. Connolly, M.F., *Fifiana* Glasgow (1869), 186

17. Lamont (1810), 161-2

18. Pryde, G.S., *The Burghs of Scotland: a critical list* London (1965)

2

Road Management and Improvement in Eighteenth-Century Fife

The Prelude to Growth

The need to provide adequate road surfaces to move agricultural products to market was given a new urgency in the early years of the eighteenth century. Since 1695 there had been a succession of years of famine, principally due to adverse weather, but exacerbated by the difficulties of distributing what food there was. Only the larger landowners were in a position to raise the capital needed to reorganise their estates for greater productivity and to invest in better roads.

Several of these men held offices of state, and had travelled to England and other countries from which they had returned infused with the spirit of agricultural improvement. Emphasis was placed on new cropping patterns and the associated need for enclosure of existing open fields, together with the planting of trees for shelter. Prominent among the pioneers of new farming in Fife was the Earl of Leven and Melville with his estate near Collessie. Sir Robert Sibbald writes in 1710 of his 'vast inclosures for pasture and barren planting'. The latter, in the form of conifer plantations, is still a distinctive feature of this part of the Howe of Fife, and today its pits for gravel and sand remind us of the barren ground beneath.

In 1703 an Act of Parliament recorded that Lord Melville, who had 'diked, ditched, hedged and planted a considerable piece of ground about the house of Melville', wished to protect a new plantation of trees. It was therefore necessary, he submitted, that the roads to the west of the house should be turned about to a line which, for the purpose of travellers, would be 'almost as near'. This represents an early stage in the process by which the somewhat random position of the highway was becoming constrained and modified by the changes in the agricultural landscape.

Large parts of Fife were, in the early eighteenth century, rendered useless for cultivation by areas of undrained marsh and accumulations of peat. The main work of draining Rossie Loch did not take place until 1741 and Sibbald refers instead to Sir William Bruce of Kinross, whose experiments in the draining of 'flow moss' had, he writes, 'made good meadow and firm ground, in which he hath raised much planting'. Draining was indeed to prove the key to the re-routing of many public roads in northern Fife, but it demanded much labour and could rarely be undertaken at a time when money was still scarce.

Sibbald also describes how, where the peat moss was sufficiently dry, 'the burning it in a drouthy and dry summer is the best mean; which my worthy friend the Lord Rankeilor performed near to his house, and made good arable and pasture ground of the moss there'.

These were just some of the activities which, in the early years of the eighteenth century, were setting the scene for radical changes in the Fife landscape along the road between Cupar and Kinross. The efforts of Lord Rankeillour's son, Thomas Hope, were to win him the Presidency of the Society of Improvers in the Knowledge of Agriculture in Scotland in 1723 when it was founded, the first agricultural society in Europe. A fellow founder member of the Society was Lord Cockburn whose instructions for repair of his estate roads were economical, if not advanced, in that they required the clearing of stones from adjacent fields, a double benefit.[1]

The Work of the Fife Commissioners of Supply

During the first quarter of the eighteenth century, whatever the initiatives taken by individual landowners on their own estates, only piecemeal repairs could be expected on public roads, the main preoccupation of the commissioners being with bridges, neglect of which would render the best of roads useless.

In the surviving Fife records,[2] which date from 1709, some of the first references are to Tower Bridge, named after the nearby eleventh-century remains and now part of Pittencrieff Park, Dunfermline. The town had grown from a defensible site in a loop of the Lyne Burn which forms a deep gorge to the west, and in 1709 the only approach to the town from that direction was over this bridge. The present structure bears the date 1788 and is probably higher than the older bridge shown in Figure 2.1. As a result there was a somewhat steeper slope up to the Abbey, and it is significant that among the extensive works undertaken by the commissioners of supply was the creation of a cutting to ease the gradient, the works being completed in 1711.[3]

Other bridges receiving attention in 1709 were those at Auchmuir, on the border with Kinross, and at Shiells, an important crossing of the

Fig. 2.1. Tower Bridge, Dunfermline. A bridge bearing the date 1611, across the Lyne Burn gorge, is said to have had two tiers of arches, even before it was rebuilt in 1788, and frequent references to it between 1709 and 1712 suggest that it was a costly structure to maintain. It is now part of a walkway through Pittencrieff Park. From an engraved view of 1690.

Eden on the old road from Kirkcaldy to Newburgh. The absence of comment by Sibbald in 1710, when describing the long-established bridges at Guardbridge, Dairsie, Cupar and over the Leven and its tributaries, matches the infrequent references to those bridges in the minutes of the commissioners, and suggests that they were well-built and in serviceable order. Indeed, it is not until 1723 that either Guardbridge or Dairsie Bridge is mentioned as in need of repair.

Repairs of roads in open country were left to the initiative of the landowners concerned, using the labour of 'the country people' as authorised by the 1669 Statute Labour Act, and few calls were made on public funds. Nevertheless, it is useful to note those cases where sums of money were being granted for road repairs, as an indication of the importance attached to such roads (or alternatively, perhaps, the opportunism of the more thrifty commissioners). Thus, at a meeting chaired by Lord Rothes in 1709, 900 merks were granted to Lord Balcarres for the building of two bridges and for repairing highways 'about Balcarres'. More specific is a payment the same year of 200 merks for repairing the Path of Kirkcaldy, 'there being a scheme produced by Sir Peter Halkett of a Method for repairing the highway in the presbytery of Kirkcaldy conform to the act of parliament'. The committee charged with the supervision of this road were recommended 'to see that the inhabitants of Kirkcaldy and Pathhead goe out and assist', in other words that they should not expect to rely on hired labour, but aim to make as much use as they could of their powers under the 1669 Act. This being a steep town road, the damage from traffic would have been severe, and it is probable that a skilled craftsman would be needed to lay a paved surface.

Most of the heavy transport on roads in Fife at this time would be of agricultural produce, but the carriage of lime as a fertiliser, and the coal with which to burn it, was becoming increasingly important. Seams of coal had been exploited landwards from the coast east of Dysart for over a century by the St Clair and Wemyss families, and as the coal was to be exported, it required little land carriage. However, coal from the oldest field in Fife near Dunfermline had long been carried for over four miles to the port of Limekilns under a duty-free privilege, renewed by parliament in 1707.[4] Lord Rothes, the chairman of the commissioners of supply in 1709, owned pits at Cluny, and needed overland transport to take his coal to Kirkcaldy harbour for export. It is perhaps not surprising that when he called on the local people to repair Cluny Bridge for this purpose, they refused and his factor had to seek a warrant to secure their compliance. His son succeeded him in 1722 and later opened fresh pits at Strathore and Cadham, bringing much coal traffic onto the road from Pittillockford (New Inn) to Kirkcaldy.

Short lengths of road in the south of the East Neuk and approaches to various bridges accounted for most of the repairs undertaken up to 1717 (Fig. 2.2), but thereafter there was an increasing tendency to authorise expenditure on substantial stretches of through roads all over Fife. These included parts of the great road between the ferries at Kinghorn on the Forth and Woodhaven on the Tay, a road of national importance, forming a link from Edinburgh to Aberdeen. Another major national route was that from Edinburgh to Inverness through Queensferry and Perth, the Great North Road. Work was done on Cantsdam Bridge in 1722, and the road from Queensferry to Inverkeithing was repaired in 1724, being extended to Crossgates the following year.

This was of course after the 1715 Jacobite Rebellion, and the commissioners would by that time be left in no doubt as to the strategic importance of this road and the need to give it a high priority in their deployment of civil resources. A plan to disarm and control the

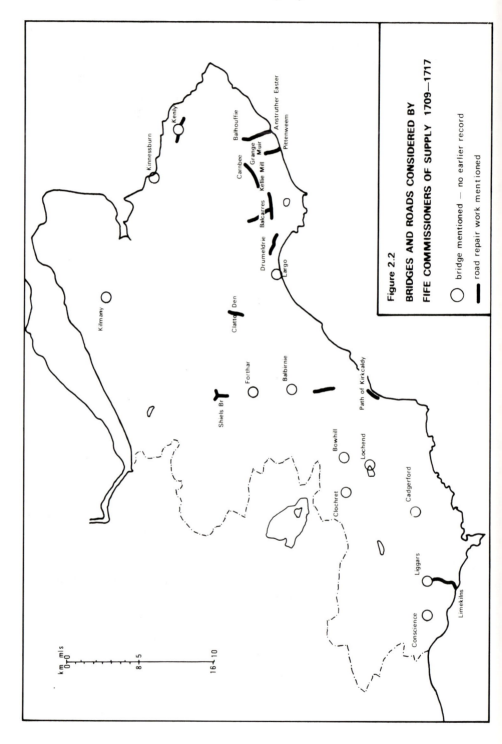

Figure 2.2

BRIDGES AND ROADS CONSIDERED BY
FIFE COMMISSIONERS OF SUPPLY 1709—1717

○ bridge mentioned — no earlier record

▬ road repair work mentioned

Highland region led to the appointment of General Wade in 1724, and it was his recommendation that led to the construction of the first new road system in Scotland since the Romans. He had originally intended to complete the road from Inverness as far south as Perth, but the existing civil road was evidently considered adequate for his purposes and the military road finished at Dunkeld, where the Inver ferry crossed the Tay.[5]

Road Technology and Improvement in Eighteenth-Century Scotland

Little is known of the technical standards to which road makers of the 1720s aspired. Wade as a young lieutenant is said to have built 'a good road for cannon' in 1708, during a campaign in Minorca,[6] and a contemporary account of his methods in the Highlands is given by Captain Burt, one of his officers.[7] The best examples of his roads do show the Roman sequence of large fitted stones, followed by smaller broken material and finished with a gravel surface, but this appears to have been the ideal rather than what was more usually accomplished. A common practice was to dig out a sixteen-foot wide trench, casting the earth into banks on either side, and filling the cavity with up to three feet of gravel. Where it was boggy, Burt records that 'the Road has been made solid by Timber and Fascines, crowned with gravel, dug out of the side of some hill'. Burt had faith in the resistance to decay of wood under boggy conditions, but where the soil was intermittently aerated, the structure was later proved to be less durable, and the road tended to become a strip of sunken marsh or even a watercourse.

Conditions in the Highlands and the speed of the work no doubt had their influence on the quality of the military roads, some of which have recently been examined in section.[8] A greater attention to detail was possible in the lowland counties when individual landowners took the initiative by building lengths of road on their estates. One of the earliest of these is recorded from the parish of Loudoun in Ayrshire, where Lord Loudoun is credited with 'the first made road in the shire' in 1731.[9] It is notable that it was from his experience as an Ayrshire road manager that a certain John Loudon McAdam later went on to a more renowned career.[10]

Elsewhere in Scotland there is evidence that the county authorities were moving from their primary concern with bridges towards programmes of road improvement. In Forfarshire attention was directed in 1736 to the road from Dundee to Brechin, and in 1739 to that from Dundee to Forfar, which had been made 'altogether impassable by the late rains'. In Perthshire, in 1736, the commissioners of supply authorised the maximum levy permitted under statute to pay for highways and bridges, and 'expected that the Justices of the Peace of the said Shire would give the proper orders'. The latter, who were in sole charge of roads, were also found to be considering improvements to the three roads radiating from Perth, together with a connection at Ardoch to the new military road from Stirling to Dalnacardoch.

Detailed records of the commissioners of supply for Fife are lacking for over thirty years after 1736, but it is an indication of the level of activity in that year that money was granted for a link from Dunfermline to the Great North Road at Beath, and for roads connecting Cupar to Newburgh and to Crail. Thereafter we have to rely on fragments of information as to what was happening in the county. The son of the Lord Rothes who had presided over the meetings in 1709 was now the appointed overseer in charge of the roads round Leslie. These included the road north from Kirkcaldy to Cupar, the southern part of which was so essential for transporting his coal from the pits at Cadham to Kirkcaldy harbour. An extract from the missing minutes for 1740, among the Rothes papers, includes a petition for the repair of this road between Waltree and Milntail (on the Pitlessie road), and also for the repair of Auchmuir Bridge.[11] Substantial repairs were also carried out along the road between the Earl's pits at Cluny and Kirkcaldy. Lord Rothes had reason to ensure that both coal roads were maintained with surfaces which would withstand traffic, composed increasingly of carts (rather than packhorses), at all seasons. Although his neighbour, Balfour of Balbirnie, also had coal pits, and was a keen rival, his support on road improvement at county meetings could be assumed. Both coal owners had an eye not only to export, but also to capture the profitable customers over the ridge in northern Fife, including the Forthar lime kilns.

Many of the road works supervised by Lord Rothes or his factor William Hay were stretches of causeway, or stone paving. This was a durable but expensive surface and in 1744 Rothes received a report of a committee on the road from Gateside, said to be in 'very bad condition'. In their opinion it would be best to 'lay the same with big stones and rubbish of quarry or gravel on the top of them . . . a ditch on each side, which would be better than a causeway, but the same could not be done by the work of the country people'. The plan they proposed would, of course, have been quite familiar to General Wade or his roadbuilding teams as it could well have described a contemporary military road. Rothes' factor commented that cause-waying when it was done made but a bad road, by which he probably meant that despite its durability a paved surface could still give a rough ride. The Earl claimed that the alternative would save the county £243 Scots and added, 'As the method is new in this county of repairing roads, it is also hoped the meeting [the commissioners of supply] will agree to allow wages to a skilfull person for directing and attending the said work'. This was a further recognition that the building or roads, as well as of bridges, could not be satisfactorily done without some specialised knowledge.

Rothes was already hiring labour rather than 'rely on the country people' in 1741, when records show his employment of 'David Jackson for twenty merks for twenty days for making the high road . . . to Kirkcaldy', and other workmen on the road to Leslie. As many as thirty-six men were employed during a period of ten days in October that year, and there are entries for the cost of mending a pick, buying a sledgehammer and wedges, and supplying nails for the wheels of a cart. For the local people doing their stint of statute labour, his expenses included such inducements as '137 pints of ale and 254 rolls', costing him £1.7.9. It is doubtful if these items were recoverable from county funds, but they were part of the jollying along which, in good weather, could perhaps turn an otherwise tiresome chore into a good-natured social event.

Post-Jacobite Recovery and Road Improvement

Following the failure of the 1745 Rebellion, the security of the Hanoverian monarchy was assured, and men of influence could concentrate their minds and capital on laying the foundations for an expanding economy. Lord Rothes, whose activities as an overseer of his district's roads continued apparently unaffected by the events of 1745-6, may have been among the more conscientious road improvers in Fife, but he was not alone: in Perthshire there was Drummond of Blair, whose father was said to have achieved little with the local labour 'though sometimes bread and ale were given by way of a premium'. The son, 'after most other men in his situation would have considered it as a thing impracticable, persevered with all that steadiness which marked his character. By a proper mixture of soothing and severity, he first brought his own tenants, and afterwards those of his neighbours, to do their duty to the roads; at last, the very servants wrought cheerfully'.[12]

The 1669 Statute Labour Act had provided guidelines only, and Ramsay of Ochtertyre, Drummond's neighbour, recalls how 'about 1747, the gentlemen of Perthshire . . . set themselves in good earnest to execute those obsolete laws'. A prominent lawyer set forth procedures for conducting the county road meetings, which 'were indeed highly respectable and well attended. And the leading men of the shire co-operated with uncommon zeal'.

Close liaison between the civil authority and the military road-builders was to be expected in Perthshire. An example had been recorded in 1743, when Major Caulfeild, Wade's successor, visited a road from Perth to Loch Tay through the Sma' Glen. It was noted that 'all the said road is being made use of for carriages, and with a little reparation may be made a very good road'.

The coast of Angus was peripheral to the military road system, but nevertheless we find in 1750 that a sum was granted to the road from Arbroath to Montrose 'to buy tools and imploying some of the military to repair the said highway'. The reasons for such cooperation are later evident in the case of the Forfar to Glamis road, the purpose being 'to make that highway more convenient for the Lords of the Justiciary in their circuit, the march of His Majesty's troops, and the lieges in the lawful trade of the country'.

In Fife, Lord Rothes in 1749 attempted to bring to the county roads some of the skills acquired by the army road teams. He asked General Churchill for a sergeant and twelve men 'to work along with the country people, which will set them an example and teach them the properest way to use their tools'.[13] He appears to have been unsuccessful, but already measures were being taken to improve the quality of statute labour after a critical reappraisal of its organisation.

In 1748 a meeting of the gentlemen of Fife in Cupar devised procedures based on the 1669 Act, designed to use to the full the supervisory skills of the landowners, and to direct the available labour and funds in the first instance to two major roads. The first was that connecting the ferry on the Forth at Kinghorn to the Tay ferry for Dundee, passing through Cupar (the present A92); the second was the branch at Pittillockford (later the New Inn junction) leading through

Falkland towards Perth (the A912).

This concentration of resources on a limited number of roads was not confined to Fife. In the Stewartry of Kirkcudbright a committee was appointed in 1749 to decide which of several tracks was to be 'the only high road' near Galloway, and again in a similar case near Dumfries. In Perthshire the Justices were asking whether money should properly be spent on the Path of Dron over the Ochils, which 'if repaired would only answer for travellers on horseback and no ways for wheel machines'. Two less steep roads were suggested as more suitable for improvement.

At the Fife meeting in 1748 a committee was appointed 'of which Lord Rothes and Lord St Clair were the spirit', to take charge of the proposed reorganisation of road repairs. Their recommendations, while upholding the existing provisions of the 1669 Act, had the ring of military authority, no doubt echoing recent experience among their number in the campaign of 1745-6. Thus, they proposed 'that each nobleman and gentleman give their attendance in their turn, from eight in the morning till five in the afternoon according to the following list, to be put into the Overseer of Road's hands, he being to write to the gentleman to be on his attendance three days before his turn is'. A list of carriages and labourers had to be presented to the Constable, noting those who had failed to turn up by ten o'clock. The list had then to be signed by the Overseer and sent to the Justices of the Peace.

The account of the 1748 proceedings is retrospective, and the writer adds, 'I must observe that it was owing to the constant and unwearied attendance of the gentlemen who had the management of these roads, animated by the example of the Lords Rothes and St Clair, that they were so well and speedily carried on, and to the employing all the county money on the most publick roads, and not parcelling it out as formerly, which was ate up by the constables without doing any good, as it was not worth any gentleman's while to attend where so few men were employed and so little to be done'.

It appears that the gentlemen did not have to keep up their rigorous duties indefinitely, for 'In five years the two great roads were finished, and the people of the country made so perfectly acquainted with that sort of work, that ever since, the roads of the county which are six . . . are carried on by a constable . . . without troubling any of the gentlemen oftener than once a fortnight to see what has been done'. At least some of the difficulties experienced by Lord Rothes in developing roadbuilding skills, with or without the help of the military, were being overcome at last. Having got the system going, the gentlemen could relax.

The identities of the extra four roads worked on between 1753 and c.1767 are not disclosed, but it would have been difficult to ignore that other national highway in the west of Fife, the Great North Road, unless they considered that its management by an independent body (see Chapter 5) excluded it from their terms of reference.

So long as haulage was carried out primarily by packhorses or by carts little larger than wheel barrows, steep slopes could be ignored, but when one road was being selected for improvement from among a number of alternatives, serious consideration was given to the reduction of gradients for wheeled loads. One commentator in 1766, believed to be Sir James Steuart of Coltness, considered that 'The statute work in some champaign counties, by the attention of the gentlemen, as in Fifeshire, has answered every purpose of its intention', and pointed out that more substantial roads were needed in more urban areas, such as Glasgow. New roads there tended to be built along the same tracks as those they replaced, and too frequently they proved to be much too steep for heavy carts. The distance travelled was less important than gradient, for 'short roads is not of so much public utility as level ones; a horse being more fatigued and strained in pulling up a steep hill of 30 or 40 yards, than if he had gone round 3 or 4 miles on a level road'.

The military roads laid out in the Highlands by Wade and his successor, Caulfeild, often exhibited that well-known characteristic of the Roman roads, a directness which tended to ignore the steepness of slopes. A working party of soldiers tended to continue a road along the bottom of a valley as far as possible and then they found themselves forced to make a steep climb. Gradients of up to 1 in 6 were constructed which were not only excessive for civil traffic, but also led to rapid erosion by rain wash of the gravel surfaces.

The critic of road alignments round Glasgow in 1766 pointed to the restrictive effects of enclosure boundaries on the freedom of roadmakers to choose more sensible lines. To make square enclosures, he said, owners had 'carried the road for some hundred yards along the side of a rising ground, or on the top of a ridge, and then turned it down a very steep hill, at a right angle, along the side of the inclosure, for a very considerable distance; and besides the bad pull produced, they added to the length of the road, as the two sides of a right angle is to the base'.

Enclosures were probably well established in Ayrshire and around

Glasgow in the late eighteenth century, as also in the Lothians, the heartland of the agricultural improvement movement. Steuart's description of Fife as a 'champaign county' in 1766 is backed up by a commentator on agricultural changes over the whole of Scotland,[14] who regards Fife as comparatively slow in the adoption of enclosures, while in 1772 Thomas Pennant remarks on the openness of the countryside along the road south of St Andrews. Straight roads were not lacking in Fife at this time, but they were more likely to have been the routes used over centuries, when a direct line saved time, even at the expense of aching muscles and shortness of breath. Among such roads, now abandoned, are those from Cupar to Newburgh over the hills, and from Kennoway to Ceres by Clatto Den.

By the time new lines of road were being considered in Fife, the disadvantages of strictly geometrical planning, or of the slavish adherence to existing routes, were coming to be recognised. On the other hand a uniform gradient was not entirely desirable, since 'horses, either in saddle or in draught, get fagged and tired when travelling always at the same pitch, even on a level, as well as on up-hill or down-hill; a variety in their pace or mode of going is more consonant to their ease. This is the opinion of those most accustomed to it — the common carriers and the stage-coachmen'.[15]

In the virtual absence of records for a road authority in Fife between 1736 and 1771, information on the development of the county's roads in this period has had to be gathered elsewhere. Fortunately, a study of the maps produced in the eighteenth century reveals a number of changes.

After the military campaigns of 1745-6 it was decided that the roadbuilding programme in the Highlands should be followed up by a survey of the whole of Scotland. This massive task was undertaken by small teams equipped with compasses and chains under the direction of William Roy, and was completed in 1755.[16] The fair copy, based on the protracted copy drawn from the field notes, provides the first comprehensive view of the road system at that date (Fig. 2.3). It has many errors and inconsistencies in detail, but the broad pattern corresponds closely to another map, again constructed without the accuracy of the triangulation method of surveying, but more carefully executed and in far greater detail. This was the map of Fife prepared by John Ainslie in 1775.

If we compare the two, we find that part of a road from Burntisland by the east shore of Loch Leven to Perth is omitted from the later map.

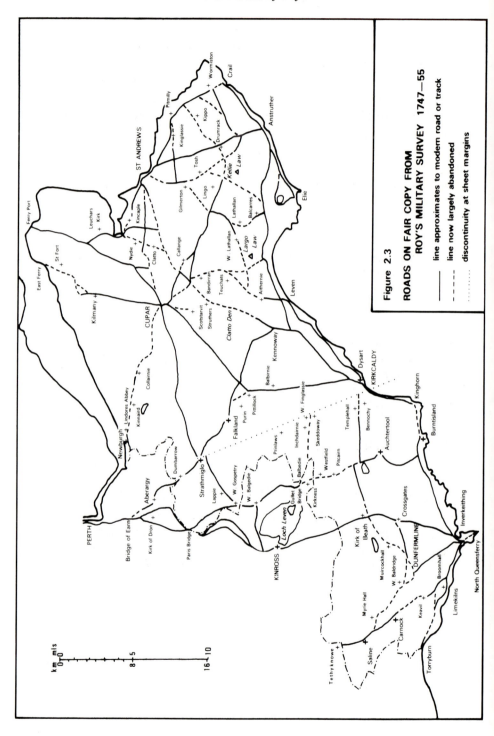

Figure 2.3

ROADS ON FAIR COPY FROM
ROY'S MILITARY SURVEY 1747—55

line approximates to modern road or track

line now largely abandoned

discontinuity at sheet margins

If this road had gone out of use between 1753, the year of the survey in Fife, and 1775, this would match the attention given to the Great North Road from Queensferry to Perth from 1753 onwards.

There is little evidence of the creation of new roads between the dates of the two maps. All the available resources under the existing system of statute labour were probably committed to upholding and improving a small selection of existing roads. However, all this was to change, and when minutes of the commissioners of supply again appear in the early 1770s, they are full of postponed decisions, pending the creation of a reformed structure and system of road management.

NOTES

1. Colville, J. (ed.), 'Letters of John Cockburn of Ormistoun to his gardener 1724-44', *Scottish History Society*, 5 (1904), 35

2. Road Authority Records, Fife Regional Council, Glenrothes

3. Chalmers, P., *Historical and Statistical Account of Dunfermline* (1844), 89

4. *O.S.A.* 311

5. Taylor, W., *The Military Roads of Scotland* (1976), 135

6. Salmond, J.B., *Wade in Scotland* (1938), 31

7. Burt, E., *Letters from a Gentleman in the North of Scotland* (1815), 281

8. Curtis, G.R., 'Roads and Bridges in the Scottish Highlands: the route between Dunkeld and Inverness, 1725-1925', *P.S.A.S.* 110 (1978-80), 475-496

9. *O.S.A.* (Ayrshire), Parish of Loudoun

10. Reader, W.J., *Macadam: The McAdam family and the Turnpike Roads 1798-1861* (1980), 27

11. Bodie, W.G.R., *Some Light on the Past around Glenrothes* (1968), 19

12. Allardyce, A. (ed.), *Scotland and Scotsmen in the Eighteenth Century*, 2 (1888), 219

13. Taylor, W. (1976), 14, note 2

14. Whittington, G. and Whyte, I.D. (eds.), *An Historical Geography of Scotland* (1983), 145

15. Robertson, G., *Rural Recollections*, Irvine (1829), 51

16. Skelton, R.A., 'The Military Survey of Scotland 1747-1755', *The Royal Scottish Geographical Society*, Special Publication No.1; Whittington, G., 'The Roy Map: The Protracted and Fair Copies', *S.G.M.*, 102 (1986), 18-28 and 66-73

3

Towards an Improved County Network

After all the effort of persuading, cajoling or even bribing the country people to turn up when required and to give of their best, even the most popular and exemplary road manager was distinctly limited in what he could expect to achieve through their labours during the six days of attendance prescribed by the 1669 Act. He knew that if money were available the hired contractor could do a much better job, and it was this knowledge that lay behind a series of local arrangements to convert labour service into monetary payments.[1]

It is true that, by the middle of the eighteenth century, there had long been the power to fine for non-attendance, but it could not be relied upon as a source of revenue and fines were notoriously difficult to collect. Substitution of money for services had been authorised in 1670 where tenants at a distance from the work could pay for workmen to take their places. In the reorganisation of statute labour in Fife in 1748 owners of small areas of pasture, who would not have been expected to employ many men or to possess carts, were allowed to pay 'twelve shillings sterling in default of the six days work of the carriage. Always providing that the aforesaid Composition Money both for day labourers and carriages be paid without trouble'.

Similar arrangements were being made in other counties, for in 1750 we find that the gentlemen of Haddingtonshire had been assessing themselves according to the 'number the several lands might reasonably keep of ploughs'. A proposal by Lord Kames in 1760 to introduce statute labour conversion elsewhere was abandoned, but Haddingtonshire secured an Act of Parliament in 1769.

Statute Labour Conversion in Fife

The corresponding Act for Fife came in 1774, and this opened a new phase in the county's road development. It was divided into the four districts of Cupar, St Andrews, Kirkcaldy and Dunfermline; the justices and commissioners of supply in each district were eligible to act as trustees, and lists of ploughgates were to be compiled. The District could decide whether, or to what extent, statute labour service would be converted, and could set its own rates 'Provided always, That the

32

aforesaid Conversion shall not exceed the ordinary Price or Rate of Labour in that Part of the Country where the Services are to be performed'.

Here was a new source of revenue to pay for skilled work where and when it was needed within the district, and not just where farmers and labourers could be persuaded to turn up on six days a year. In addition, the maximum county tax on valued rent was doubled to twenty shillings Scots in one hundred pounds (£12 Scots was equivalent to £1 sterling), most of which would be spent on district bridges, any expenditure in excess of fifty pounds sterling being shared with other districts.

In the two years before the 1774 Act was passed, a brief glimpse is given of road administration under the county commissioners of supply. The business conducted is in the nature of a holding operation, as it is obvious from their referral of numerous petitions to the first forthcoming district meeting that they have no wish to take on any responsibilities that can be passed on to the new bodies. Few records survive for districts in Fife other than Cupar between 1774 and 1790, and this may perhaps be explained by the primacy of Cupar itself as the county town and seat of legal administration. Indeed, the town was clearly conscious of the need to set an example, as in 1790, when for the first mile on either side of the town along the road from Dundee to Kinghorn the width was to be 30 feet, that is to say 14 feet built with stones with a 3 feet margin, leaving 13 feet for a summer road: 'as it is near so public a Town . . . it should be done in the most perfect manner'. Fortunately it was also the hub of the road network in northern Fife, so that the developments recorded reveal much of what was happening in the county as a whole.

One of the few new road-works known to have been undertaken by St Andrews district before 1790 comes to light through a retrospective claim made to the commissioners of supply in 1784. William Thomson of Priorletham (497127) complained that he had not been adequately compensated for the land taken for a road made some ten years earlier from St Andrews to Colinsburgh, Elie and Largo. He also claimed the cost of the stone dykes he was obliged to build on either side of the road in 1783. The commissioners had to tell him that the petition did not 'properly come before them'. The fact that Thomson was misinformed suggests that either he was surprisingly ignorant as to how roads were managed in the St Andrews district, or that their activities were minimal.

On 14th June 1774 the new statute labour road trustees for Cupar

District met to appoint committees to supervise each of nineteen listed roads. Another committee was to meet representatives of St Andrews District to agree on repairs to Dairsie Bridge, which was a shared responsibility. Of the six days' labour service prescribed by the 1669 Act, only two were to be converted to money, and the rates of 4d per labourer and 20d per cart were charged for each day. The tax on valued rent was to remain, for the time being, at the previous 10s in £100, there being a slight surplus from the previous year.

A second meeting on 12th July resolved 'to tell precentors from the Letterons [lecterns] of Parish Churches on Sunday . . . to dismiss their congregations after morning service, so that conversion money may be paid to constables or overseers appointed by the different committees'. The constables were not entirely successful, it seems, for in August trustees from North Fife secured warrants from justices to recover unpaid conversion money, and a certain constable was later reported 'to be incarcerate in the Tollbooth of Cupar' until the money was paid, and then for a further eight days.

The traditionally independent weavers of Auchtermuchty refused in 1792 to give either statute labour service or pay conversion money. It was therefore proposed that 'a clever active messenger should be employed to put warrants into execution'. If 'deforced', the trustees would apply for military assistance.

The Roads to Newburgh

A certain continuity can be seen in the priorities accepted by the new road managers for Fife, particularly in respect to the routes connecting Edinburgh through the Broad Ferry to Perth via Newburgh and to Dundee via Cupar.

Just before the 1774 Act had been passed there had been a flood of petitions to the former road authority, the county commissioners of supply, from landowners and merchants, no doubt hoping to be at the head of the queue when money was to become available to carry out road improvements. When consideration of roads within Cupar District began, it was the two 'great roads' on which the county's resources had first been concentrated in 1748, that received the greatest attention: the road from Kinghorn through Cupar to the Dundee ferries, and its branch towards Perth. The latter was supported by an eloquent petition from the heritors and linen dealers of Auchtermuchty, who stressed the

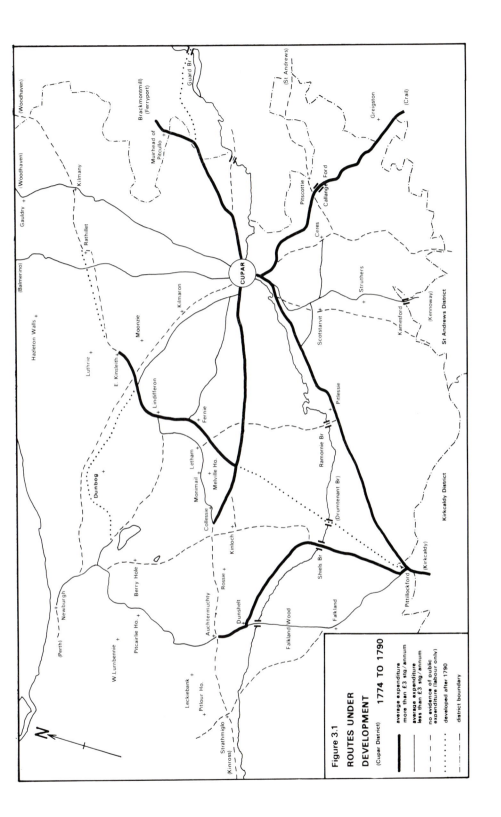

Figure 3.1

ROUTES UNDER
DEVELOPMENT

(Cupar District)   1774 TO 1790

	average expenditure more than £3 stg/annum
	average expenditure less than £3 stg/annum
	no evidence of public expenditure (labour only)
	developed after 1790
	district boundary

need for a bridge at Dunshelt. This, they said, would lead 'southward to the Coals, Lyme and Coast of Fife and northwards to Newburgh, the nearest market for wood and iron, where most of the linen bought at Auchtermuchty and Strathmiglo and . . . great quantities of flax and yarn is weekly landed from Dundee for the use of the manufacturers in the neighbourhood'.

Others, however, wanted to repair the existing bridge over the Eden at Shiells (Fig. 3.1), rather than build not only a new bridge at Dunshelt but also an expensive new road over low-lying ground northwards from Falkland. Access to the port of Newburgh was desired by the people of Falkland for whom the route via Shiels Bridge had seemed unnecessarily long. They represented that not only would there be 'a great advantage to Linnen manufacturers, as the greatest part of the Linnens made in Falkland and neighbourhood are brought to Auchtermuchty for sale', but that the saving of three miles by a road through Falkland Wood could benefit Newburgh, since 'all the imports and exports presently carried on in the Parish of Falkland and neighbourhood are made at the port of Kirkcaldy'.

The people of Falkland had their way, for the new road was staked out in 1784. The Shiels Bridge road was also improved, because it remained the principal route for through traffic between Kirkcaldy and Newburgh and, by a branch at Kinloch, a means of reaching Dundee through the hills of northern Fife. In 1785 it was claimed that as many as two hundred carriages could pass over the bridge in a day, presumably during the season for driving lime and coal from the south.

While Auchtermuchty might be solving the problem of supplies from Kirkcaldy, there still remained difficulties of access to Newburgh. To the north the hills were crossed by a number of rough tracks, some so ill-defined that affidavits were required from local inhabitants to establish their existence.

North of Auchtermuchty a road was staked out as far as Broombrae (240124) in 1774. The route beyond was controversial, for there appears to have been some local confusion at this time over the status of certain roads to the north of Strathmiglo and Auchtermuchty. In 1775 residents of both towns complained that what they termed 'the Great Road to Newburgh' had been 'turned about' by Baxter or Leckiebank to go round his enclosures. Trustees were told that this had happened some years previously and that the road was now 'absolutely impassable'. A month later Mr Baxter replied to the meeting that in his opinion the road to Newburgh went through Auchtermuchty 'which is now repairing in a compleat manner at a great expense to the County as a proper highway'. What he referred to snidely as 'the said Track, now christened the great road from Strathmiglo to Newburgh' or 'this bye way' had, he claimed, been seldom used except by the owners of Pitlour and Pitcairlie when visiting one another. The previous owner of his land had established its status as a 'road by tolerance' and, to confirm that status, had ploughed over it once a year. Baxter had not continued this practice, and he now claimed that not only was the diversion he had made for his enclosures in a better state than the original road, but that it was 'not confined to any breadth . . . and the foord at the bottom is well filled up with stones'.

As to the road northward from Broombrae, the trustees considered three alternative lines for improvement: through Wester Lumbenny (227157), by Haltonhill (245162) or by Berryhole (258159), of which the second was judged the best. Three years later, however, the exact line was still undetermined and, since at this time a road was a somewhat vague entity, perhaps existing in the mind rather than in reality, a resident was induced to make a 'deposition'. He had lived in the vicinity since 1732 and considered that there was no established road on the east side of the burn, that carts travelling from Lumbenny to Auchtermuchty came across the burn, 'sometimes on Mr Cheape's ground and sometimes on Mr Cathcart's ground', and then kept to the channel of the burn till they came to the Whitefield or common; that about six or seven years previously the burn was straightened, 'and this truth as he shall answer to God'. After hearing another witness the trustees concluded that there was no fixed road on the east side of the burn by the back of the house of Lumquhat Miln, but that there was an established road from the Whitefield or Commonty up the burn. It was agreed to stake out a line for this road. This was done, but in the face of complaints from local linen dealers that the road would be too steep. Only modest funds were allocated to the road, and in spite of vigorous efforts by the landowner, it was to be another twenty years before what became known as the Pitcairlie road was completed. This is but one of many instances in which it can be shown how what have now become important main roads owe their initial planning to quite arbitrary decisions on the part of a committee of three or four trustees. Its role as a turnpike road and as a regular stage-coach route will be described in Chapters 5 and 6.

From Cupar there were three ways to Newburgh. One was along the old road to Kinross, branching off at Kinloch over a hill road past

Black Loch. A second way was through Fernie and over the hills to Lindores Loch, a steep and exposed route (Fig. 5.7). The third lay along the northern side of a long depression approached through Kilmaron, passing Moonzie Kirk and, after going through Balmeadowside and Glenduckie, climbing over Lindores Hill opposite Dunbog to reach Newburgh. It is an indication of the forward planning of what was to become a fast motor road, that the transfer of this hillside road to the valley bottom was already in hand in 1782 under a 'Cupar to Kilmaron and Moonzie' committee, who were able to secure extra carriages from the statute labour trustees for work on the road. In 1790 a series of allocations were made from the available labourers of Newburgh, at the other end of the same road, but not without protest. In the opinion of the citizens of that burgh the high street, 'the great through-fare twixt the County of Perth and the heart of Fife . . . was much resorted to from the Country about by Gentlemen, farmers and others shipping victual at the Shores of Newburgh and driving wood and other merchandise therefrom'. Why, they asked, should their statute labour be applied to roads with which they had no concern, when at the same time their own street was allowed to go 'into total disrepair'? As a compromise they were to be allowed to use the labour of sixty inhabitants to repair the streets of the town.

Roads to the Dundee Ferry

Perhaps the most far-sighted of the schemes initiated by the Cupar statute labour trustees was the establishment of a valley route between what is now known as the Melville gates (304127) through Lindifferon towards Dundee.[2] This would avoid going through Cupar and would take advantage of lower gradients, a consideration which was becoming increasingly important to the carters carrying loads from the 'coalhills of Balbirnie and Cadham' and the 'limekilns of Forthar' — all near the Pittillockford junction. Whether the later Drumtenant Bridge route was envisaged at this stage is uncertain, but it would certainly have been a bold undertaking, on the revenue of the statute labour conversion alone.

In 1776 the road committee under its convener, Robert Baillie of Luthrie, reported that two years' work had already been done, resulting in the completion of 3,000 yards of road, and they were now asking for £15 towards the cost of another 2,000 yards, including the paving of a ford. Beyond Luthrie, two routes were being supported by allocation of extra carriages, under the supervision of a committee for a road 'from Woodhaven to Kinghorn by Lythrie', and another for a 'Kinsleith and Lindifferon Road'. From this it would seem that the normal route to Woodhaven was not along the valley bottom where Easter Kinsleith is now situated (333185), but over the hills through Hazleton Walls (338221).

At the same time the older route through Cupar was not being neglected. The connection to the north to the Dundee ferries over the hills via Kilmany had long been criticised for its steep climbs, and as early as 1730 funds were being allocated to an alternative lower route by Pitcullo. In 1779 much still needed to be done to the latter road, since it was described as 'much broke in many places about Dron Muir'. The nearby Pittormie Bridge was said to be undermined by the burn and it was decided to replace the bridge by one which was wider and better aligned with the direction of the road to Brackmontmill. Between 1774 and 1790 this road was to receive a total of £104 up to 1790, whereas the Balmerino road got £30 and the Kilmany road only £14 during the same period.

Districts were generally regarded as self-sufficient, but in the case of this road, often referred to as 'The Great Road through Fife', Kirkcaldy was approached for assistance and, in its turn, Cupar contributed towards the ferry at Pettycur, further confirmation of the status of the road as a major highway.

Roads to the South and to the Broad Ferry

The Great Road connecting Cupar to the Broad Ferry (the collective title of the group of ferry ports comprising Burntisland, Pettycur, Kinghorn and Kirkcaldy) went through Pitlessie and the important junction which lay between the Lomond Hills and the East Fife hills at Pittillockford.

The section which lay in Cupar district was generously supported with funds, as is indicated in Figure 3.1, for there would have been complaints from Kirkcaldy and Dundee, or even Edinburgh and Aberdeen, if the road had been neglected. It was, of course, one of the two principal roads on which it had been decided in 1748 to concentrate the resources of the whole county (p. 26). Nevertheless, the support was from time to time shown to be inadequate, as in 1786,

Fig. 3.2. The old Kennoway to Cupar road down Garley Bank. The direct way down to Tarvit Mill is marked by the line of trees crossing the Ceres to Pitlessie road. The curved fence line follows the less steep road towards Cupar.

when a farmer at Pitlessie claimed compensation for damage to his clover crop, on account of the road having become quite impassable and traffic making a detour through his fields, a reminder that by this time enclosure of arable land and the growth of valuable crops could make failure to maintain a hard road expensive for the trustees.

Another way to Kinghorn from Cupar had long been the road directly over the east-west ridges of the East Neuk towards Kennoway. The steepness of the old road up Garley Bank and past Scotstarvit can still be seen (Fig. 3.2), and a terraced approach to the crossing of the burn in Clatto Den did not entirely remove the problem of negotiating the steep sides. Funds were withdrawn from this road, to the chagrin of heritors such as Gourlay of Craigrothie, who claimed in 1787 that for ten years, as convener of the Scotstarvit road committee, he 'had not been allowed a single carriage or a half penny' for a road which 'ran through the petitioner's lands at the very door of his farmstead'. An active trustee, Captain Wemyss, who lived at Wemyss Hall (now Hill of Tarvit House), made sure that a regular sum was expended on the road past the entrance to his house on the road between Ceres and Pitlessie. This would not have pleased his neighbour, Gourlay, with his

Scotstarvit road in a state of neglect, but for some years the bulk of the carriages and labour were diverted to a road which brought Gourley even less benefit, the road from Cupar to the coast towns of south-east Fife.

Although a new route was being considered, passing east of Struthers and crossing the Clatto Burn at Kames, as early as 1775, it was not in fact until after 1790 that it was completed, and progress in the building for this important road will be described in Chapter 5.

The Crail Road

Just as the more modern line of road to the Tay ferry through Pitcullo grounds was being actively supported in the 1730s, so also was the road to the south-east, to Crail. One reason was that it led not only to Crail but 'to the coalside', for here, in the neighbourhood of Greigston (451113), were coal pits supplying Cupar. The section between Callange Ford (415125) and the east end of Bruntshiels Moss (450104) was the subject of expenditure as early as 1736, and one of its purposes

Fig. 3.3. The old Cupar to Crail road. The line of trees over the skyline, right, marks the course of the road from Cupar, now replaced by a road through Pitscottie, passing behind the observer.

Fig. 3.4. Abandoned bridge at Callange. This substantial structure was built in the late 18th century, but was made redundant by the switch of traffic to the new Pitscottie road (No. 14) before 1817.

was to provide an alternative route from Cupar to Crail to that through Ceres, with its steep slopes on either side of the Ceres Burn. The road between Ceres Muir and Pitscottie was begun in 1784 and by 1787 extended for six miles from Cupar, as far as Greigston. This progress was made possible by a series of transfers of statute labour, not only from neighbouring parts of Cupar district, but by means of reciprocal arrangements with St Andrews. The easily accessible coal seams along this road may have encouraged the relatively high level of expenditure which was sustained for sixteen successive years. How far the road was improved through the St Andrews district in the direction of Crail at this stage is uncertain, but the eastern sections of it were still below a standard suitable for a toll road some fifty years later.

The stretch between Ceres Muir and Callange Ford (Figs. 3.3 and 3.5) was soon to be replaced by a new road through Pitscottie. Since a substantial bridge had been built to replace the ford before the old road was abandoned (Fig. 3.4), this would mean that such expenditure had been short-sighted. Beyond Callange the Crail road gave access to further coal supplies by a branch to Drumcarrow, where remains of small family workings are still being discovered, and to the lime quarry

Fig. 3.5. Approaches to Cupar in 1775. John Ainslie's map shows the old Crail road through Sodom, and the three roads climbing to Scotstarvit on the road through Chance Inn and Clatto (Claret) Den to Kennoway and Leven. He also shows the St Andrews road over Dairsie Bridge (Fig. 9.9) via Chapel Well.

at Ladeddie. This was built as a through road towards St Andrews in 1785, the two districts sharing the cost (Fig. 3.6).

The allocation of resources to the Crail road, of which Gourlay of Craigrothie had complained, was only temporary, and by 1787 they were again switched back to a road west of Ceres; this time not to the now abandoned Scotstarvit road but to the new, skilfully engineered road to Kennoway through Kamesford, the present A916. Predictably, just as Gourlay had complained about the transfer of statute labour, so representatives of St Andrews district, through which the Crail road passed, made their protest. General Durham of Largo wrote in 1787 to

Fig. 3.6. An old coal and lime road to Cupar. The coal pits were to the south (right) of Drumcarrow Craig. To the left were the lime kilns of Laddedie. The road was continued towards St Andrews by the district trustees in 1785, but was replaced by a turnpike road (No. 80) past Craigtoun before 1833.

the convener of the Cupar trustees, and memorials were received from the Earl of Kellie, Sir Robert Anstruther, Mr Bethune of Kilconquhar and Mr Patullo of Balhouffie, saying that the road 'from Cupar to the Coastside' would be completed in two years as far as Greigston (the boundary with St Andrews district) and that 'In order to be a saving to the Cupar District by turning the Coast and Ceres into one, a new line through the Muir was begun three years ago, but one year after, the carriages were taken away to some road by Scotstarvit'.

Without this supply of transport from local farms they were unable to proceed, the remaining 'carriages' being inadequate for the six miles of road they were intending to improve. The Cupar trustees relented and allowed some of the transport to continue to be allocated to the St Andrews road, in spite of their heavy commitment to the road to Kennoway.

Management Skills

For much of the period 1774 to 1790, a prominent figure among the Cupar trustees was Robert Baillie of Luthrie. Trained as an assistant in a firm of Edinburgh merchants, he later managed the family estate in the absence of his brother, a senior army officer. He devoted much of his time to roads in northern Fife and by 1786 was convener of six out of the twenty road committees for the Cupar district. The following year he made several proposals to the trustees, including the appointment of a single person to direct and manage the roads, a suggestion readily taken up, with no better candidate than himself.

His reports on the condition of the roads and the trust's expenditure are impressive for the time, and in 1789 he circulated a list of questions to the trustees on such matters as the use of town carts for road repairs (Q.1), apportionment of rates after transfers of land (Q.2), the liability for labour service of tradesmen (Q.3), interpretation of the law with regard to standard road widths (Qs.5 and 6), control by landowners of watercourses where they affected roads (Qs.4 and 7), and a landowner's obligation to make up a diverted section of road to an acceptable standard (Q.8) [or, in full:] 'When a proprietor applys for streightning a road, tho' not materially turned, but so as the new road requires to be carefully formed and covered, is the public or the proprietor to be at the expence?

This being the last query, the minute continues (and the complete answers are given, providing, as they do, a rare glimpse of the detail of road management): 'Which queries above written having been read and considered by the Meeting, they are of the opinion as to query 1: That all Carts not kept for hyre, however triffling is the ground they possess, to be rated at half a plough or three days work. As to query 2: The Occupier to be taxed at the same rate, until he gets a disjunction, either by bargain, or by the Justices. As to query 3: The same ought to be enforced, particularly after the determination of the quarter Sessions, which was that all Tradesmen of whatever denomination were liable, who were not hyred by the year for a specific wage. As to query 4: No person can bring any run of water upon the highroad, or they are liable to every damage and to every expence of preventing its doing any. As to query 5: 25 feet clear of ditches or water runs, where necessary. As to query 6: All roads that get Statute labour are public roads, and where they can be made 25 feet ought to be so. As to query 7: It is the practice in St Andrews district and must be enforced in this district. As to query 8: If altered, to be made as good as the old road, that no additional expence be laid on the public, for any man's conveniency or fancy'.

His concern to get to grips with these problems marks Baillie as an active and conscientious road manager, but his enthusiasm was not universally shared, as was shown by a motion put to the trustees by Kinnear of Kinloch in April 1790 'that it is the opinion of this meeting that an office of inspector for the roads as appointed by this District these last two years, is found highly improper and expensive, as well as useless, and that this District ought not again to agree to such an office being established'. No vote is recorded, but in May a meeting decided not to appoint a general overseer for the following year.

Baillie may have been too energetic for the peace of mind of some trustees, but a more practical reason for the decision was that most of the major roads could, following the passage of the 1790 Turnpike Act, be managed by a full-time surveyor, who would be a servant rather than a tiresome equal.

However much an individual trustee might try to increase the efficiency of road management under the statute labour system, there were limits imposed by the apathy of the less-motivated trustees, expressed as slack book-keeping, procrastination, and even deliberate obstruction by certain of the more awkward members. In short, the limitations were largely those of human nature.

Faced as the road trustees were with these difficulties, the greater capital investment made available by resort to the charging of tolls, already established across the western end of the county, was one, and perhaps the only, means of escape.

NOTES

1. Whetstone, A.E., *Scottish County Government in the Eighteenth and Nineteenth Centuries* Edinburgh (1981), 86

2. The normal ferry was at Woodhaven. Later Newport became more important (Chapter 8).

4

Turnpike Roads: Their Introduction to Scotland

The charging of tolls to pay for the upkeep of bridges and short sections of road had, by the early eighteenth century, been long established in Scotland. An Act of Parliament in 1593 was intended 'to repair, beit and mend the Calsey betvix his maiesties palice yett [gate] of haliruidhous and the nether bow of Edinburgh'. A less specific purpose was assigned to a toll on roads to the south and east of Edinburgh at Liberton in 1661, when the money was to be applied to both bridges and highways within that parish.

These were roads in or near towns where heavy traffic would give rise to expensive repairs. Out in the countryside such arrangements continued to be rare, one recorded exception being the upkeep of the Causey Mounth on the main coast road south of Aberdeen, for the benefit of which tolls were authorised by several Acts of Parliament between 1597 and 1669.

By the latter date, more comprehensive experiments were being conducted in England under what came to be known as the 'turnpike' road system, after the horizontal barrier which could be swung aside after tolls had been paid. After attempts at legislation in 1609 and 1621, the first English turnpike act was passed in 1663, for a toll road in Hertfordshire. Further turnpike roads followed from 1694 onwards, and by the end of the century a network had rapidly developed across England.[1]

First in Scotland to be turnpiked were the roads within the County of Edinburgh which were the subject of an Act in 1713. The trustees appointed were the justices of the peace from that county, and they were authorised to erect an unspecified number of tollbars; only goods traffic was to be charged. Riders and passenger vehicles were exempted from tolls, and this accords with the spirit of the opening words: 'Whereas the Supreme Courts of Judicature, and the chief officers for collecting and managing Her Majesty's Revenues . . . do sit and meet at the city of Edinburgh . . .' Thus the arrangement appears to have been to use the money paid by tradesmen to make travel more pleasant for the powerful. Indeed, a local citizen was to remark, over a century later, 'Perhaps there never was a more unblushing assumption of privilege'.[2] The Act did not identify the roads from which tolls were to

Fig. 4.1. Old post road, Berwick to Edinburgh. The road followed the slopes of the
Garleton Hills north of Haddington, and the concentrated traffic creating this hollow
way would have been taking the lowest route to pass above the enclosure dyke, right.

be collected, but a map assigned to 1759 shows three tollbars.[3]

In England there had been a period of over thirty years between the
first and subsequent acts, and similarly it was not until 1750 that
further Scottish turnpike roads were authorised. As might be expected,
the next roads to be the subject of turnpike acts were those radiating
from Edinburgh towards London, Glasgow and the north. The great
post road through Berwick had changed parts of its course several times
over the centuries. That section from Ayton over Coldingham Moor,
criticised by the Privy Council in 1617, is still passable in a vehicle
today, but the old road passing north of Haddington was to be replaced
by one through the town itself. The Act, said to be 'for repairing the
roads leading from Dunglass Bridge to the town of Haddington, and
from thence to Ravensburgh-burn', referred to 'the greatest Post Road
from Edinburgh to London', which was 'by reason of the deepness of
the Soil and the many heavy Carriages passing along the same, in many
Parts ruinous, and so much out of Repair, that Travellers [could not]
pass thereon without great Danger'. Certainly, the presence of hollow
ways such as that illustrated in Figure 4.1 confirms the pressing need

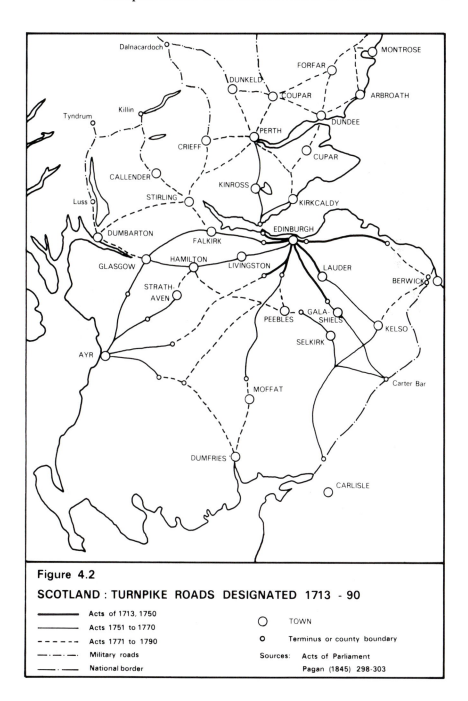

Figure 4.2

SCOTLAND : TURNPIKE ROADS DESIGNATED 1713 - 90

———— Acts of 1713, 1750	○ TOWN
———— Acts 1751 to 1770	
– – – – – Acts 1771 to 1790	● Terminus or county boundary
–·—·—·— Military roads	Sources: Acts of Parliament
—·—·— National border	Pagan (1845) 298-303

for a solidly constructed road, and the steep climbs over the Garleton Hills would have become increasingly unpopular as the size of vehicles increased.

Further tolls were authorised for roads from Edinburgh to Queensferry in 1751 and to Glasgow via Falkirk in 1752. An alternative southerly route to Glasgow through Livingston followed in 1753, together with the road through Carlops towards Dumfries and Carlisle (Fig. 4.2). The turnpiking of the connection to Queensferry was just the first stage in improving the vital link to Inverness, the Great North Road; this crossed the western end of Fife, permission to erect toll-gates on the section to Perth being granted in 1753.

For tolls to be exacted from road users a certain minimum standard of reliability and evenness of running surface was regarded as essential, and this standard was higher than could be expected from the limited resources provided by statute labour or its monetary equivalent. Investment in a road to be turnpiked could be secured on the anticipated revenue of the tollbars at a fixed rate of interest, usually five per cent. There were benefits to landowners in the provision of better roads from the reduction of the marketing costs of their tenants, thus enabling them to increase rents; also from increased profits from the sale of coal and other minerals present on their estates.

As was noted earlier, much prestige attached to the improvement of roads, especially where they were of both local and national benefit; to figure prominently in a list of subscribers was a desirable object in itself, particularly where the chances of access to public office might be enhanced. The Queensferry to Perth road was part of a national through route for which trustees were named in the Act from the counties of Fife, Kinross and Perthshire. Of the sixty-nine trustees from Fife, over half resided in the districts of Cupar and St Andrews, where the preferred route to Edinburgh would have been by way of the Broad Ferry from Kinghorn; only a handful attended the meetings of the Great North Road Trust, which were often held at Kinross or Perth. Those who did attend, however, were to form a nucleus of informed and experienced road managers, able at a later date to influence their fellow heritors when an extension of the system into the rest of Fife came to be considered.

After a lull of eleven years, the number of roads designated under successive turnpike acts grew rapidly and there was what might be described as the counterpart of the 'turnpike boom' that had taken place in England in the early 1700s. Between 1764 and 1789 some eighteen new turnpike bills were passed, mostly designating several roads within a particular county, but some, such as that for the turnpiking of the remaining stretch of the London road between Dunglass Bridge and Berwick, for one road only. A distinction should be made between roads listed in a turnpike act, some of which may have been little more than pious hopes, and those actually improved to turnpike standard and provided with tollgates. As will be seen in the case of Fife, the proportion of unfulfilled designations was often as high as a quarter.

Enclosures and the Choice of Alignments

One of the most active areas of turnpike road development was Strathclyde, where some twelve roads had been listed in acts in 1753, as compared with five in the rest of Scotland for that year. In a pamphlet of 1766, the presumed author, Sir James Steuart of Coltness, reviewed the progress of road improvement round Glasgow and between the Firth of Clyde and the Forth. He was greatly concerned at what he considered a widespread failure of the recently appointed turnpike road trustees to choose more suitable lines for the roads listed in the various acts. Such failures could be most damaging to commerce, he claimed, by adding unnecessarily to the cost of transport.

He contrasted the situation in Fife, where 'the statute work [had] answered every purpose of its intention', with that around large towns such as Glasgow, where it was impossible, with statute labour alone, 'to make roads fit to support heavy carriages'. Fife, where in 1753 the Great North Road had been turnpiked, he described as a 'champaign' county, that is to say the building of dykes and fences to create enclosures was as yet little advanced, and this, he said, meant that 'wheel carriages . . . could pass along in many different roads in the same direction'. In other words, room being available for several more or less parallel tracks, the damage done by traffic could be spread over a broad band of ground.

'Although', he says, 'the old line of road, when it was first formed, was judicious, and the only possible way that individuals could have intercourse with each other, . . . what was proper in the state of a country uncultivated and almost devoid of trade and commerce, was very injudicious and improper of late years, when both were arrived to a considerable height'.

The making of enclosures, while in many places doubling or tripling the value of the land, had 'very bad effects in the direction of the roads in many places', and had, as we saw in Chapter 2, the effect of introducing steeply sloping diversions and increasing the distance. The gentlemen concerned had not 'apprehended the damage they were doing their country, in terms of increasing the cost of transport', and Steuart notes that 'in this situation were many parts of the principal roads in Scotland when the gentlemen applied to Parliament for turnpikes'. The road trustees, 'residing on their estates, and many of them having no occasion to travel through England', did not have the experience to understand the spirit of the new turnpike acts and the powers with which they were vested, particularly the power to deviate from routes which, as expressed in the acts, were descriptive rather than prescriptive. They therefore felt obliged to keep as near as possible to a line originally 'chosen by the farmer and carrier over hills and alongst the higher parts of the champaign grounds; the country being uncultivated, and having no drains to carry off the moisture'.

One deficiency common to the early turnpike bills noted by Steuart was their failure to require an adequate minimum width for a road. It had been set at twenty feet under previous legislation, 'which was sufficiently wide at that time for the summer season'. As he points out, 'The whole country was open, after the crop was separated from the ground, [and] they could leave the high road at pleasure, and follow any direction that was more commodious; there being no carts and waggons at that time, the whole produce being carried on horseback, and twenty feet was then sufficient to let a coach or rider pass carriers' horses or horses loaded with grain'. Thus, the denial of the freedom to seek alternative routes through the building of enclosure dykes meant that a width of forty feet was now desirable.

Late Eighteenth-Century Road Planning in Scotland

Steuart was not alone as an advocate of new principles of road alignment. Sir George Clerk of Penicuik, who died in 1784, was described as 'the first man in Scotland who appears to have conceived the idea of conducting roads through hilly and mountainous districts with a systematic attention to the most level direction',[4] and he seems to have inspired Lord Daer, the son of a landowner in Galloway. After having 'met with much obstruction from the prejudices and contracted views of many of the country gentlemen whose concurrence was necessary for effecting his plans', Lord Daer in the 1780s laid out roads with easier gradients within his father's estate, 'without interfering with the lands of other proprietors who might not be disposed to promote them'. These roads proved not only more convenient but diminished the expense of repair by being shorter. It was several years before he could win the cooperation of the gentlemen of Galloway 'to execute a few miles of a public road in a distant part of the country; nor', he complained, 'was this obtained without a pecuniary sacrifice on his part'. The required parliamentary bill by this time encountered little opposition from the owners of land along its route, for they had 'the prospect of so great an increase in the value of their property that few of them were disposed to give much obstruction to the making of the road in any line most advantageous to the public'.

It can be seen that in the years before the first turnpike bill was envisaged for the county of Fife as a whole, much had been learned, both from the English experience and from the debate in other parts of Scotland, that was to benefit the planning of new roads in that county. The mistakes of sticking to traditional routes selected in former centuries for less demanding traffic, the temptation to set out straight lines across the landscape regardless of gradients, and the diversion of public roads round the corners of square enclosures: all these evils could be avoided with a little care.

Apart from the 1753 Act for the Queensferry to Perth Road, the Scottish turnpike acts up to 1788 were all for roads south of the River Forth, but in 1789 and 1790, acts were passed for the counties of Perth, Stirling, Forfar and Fife. The first three counties designated roads up to their borders, to be continued as turnpikes into the adjacent counties. As will be seen in the next chapter, the network of Fife turnpike roads was developed initially within the limits set by the two firths, and roads in the 1790 Act were only vaguely directed towards a link-up with their counterparts to the west.

Roadbuilding Technology

A body of knowledge in the field of road construction and maintenance had been building up, over the years, since the days when commissioners of supply looked to the military road builders as a source of expertise or even of skilled labour. Recommendations from those gentlemen managing roads and from the emerging breed of professionals, the road surveyors, showed a great diversity. In England a notable pioneer was John Metcalf, blind from the age of six, who nevertheless became a national figure in road construction. After a brief attempt to introduce a vehicle hire service in Harrogate, he joined a local company of volunteers at the time of the 1745 rebellion and became indispensable as a fiddler. The company marched to join General Wade's army, retired from the defeat at Falkirk to Edinburgh, and finally set out to confront the rebels at Culloden in 1746.[5]

Marching over highland roads, constructed at an earlier date by his commanding officer, it would have been strange if Metcalf had not thought long and hard about road construction. On leaving the army he set himself up as a carrier in Yorkshire. In 1765, when a turnpike act was passed for a local road, he won a contract for building a three-mile section. This was only the first of a long line of commissions in counties of northern England, and his ability to judge the nature of the ground and the best use of local materials became a legend. It may not be a coincidence that he chose to use a raft of brushwood to float a road on a deep bog, the same method as had been described by Burt when serving under General Wade.[6]

Around Glasgow, Sir James Steuart of Coltness, whose strong views on the planning of routes for new turnpike roads we noted, was also concerned to improve standards of road maintenance. He considered that roads, even when paved with 'whin or gray prophyry', could not resist the damage done by carters, 'who seldom or never quarter their ground, if they can find an old tract or rut to go in', and cited a case of hard pavement cut into gutters six inches deep. 'There is nothing', he writes, 'more injudicious than the usual practice, in this country, of leaving the turnpike roads uncovered, by which means the carriages, in a few years, cut through the foundation'. His remedy was to require a road contractor to employ a man on a stretch of up to four miles with a hand cart 'to fill up all ruts and such places as water could settle on. By this means it would always be kept dry, and not liable to be broke into holes as all roads must necessarily be'. A contractor, in his opinion, should be paid, not per mile of road, but 'by the cart or waggon load of materials he laid on it'. Significantly, Steuart makes no requirement as to the nature of the materials to be applied, and his apparent indifference to what was to become a crucial element in road technology may be compared with the strictures on inferior roadstone which occur in trustees' reports of later years.

In a report of 1788 to a Fife county road committee the surveyor stressed the necessity for stones to be the hardest available. These 'should be all broke before they are laid on, the largest of them not to exceed two and a half inches thick and three inches broad'. Gravel (smaller stones) could be used provided that all sand and earth were removed. That the importance of stone size was becoming widely recognised at this time is made evident by an excavation of a road built in 1779. This showed the selection of stones of the size later required by McAdam.

When that former Ayrshire road trustee set out to find an economical method of road construction and maintenance, he drew upon the experience of numerous road overseers, contractors and surveyors both in Scotland and in England. From his inquiries McAdam developed his famous method, one of the principal features of which was the abandonment of large fitted blocks as a foundation and reliance on a uniform body of hard angular stones of strictly controlled dimensions. His argument was based on the area of contact between a wheel and the road surface. Too small a stone would be crushed, while a stone which was too large he termed 'mischievous', since it would either roll rather than be pressed in or, if it resisted the wheel, would cause it to drop hard after passing over it and make a depression. McAdam favoured a standard six-ounce stone, 'the size of a hen's egg', of tough rock, broken with a hammer of specified weight and placed in rolled layers to a depth of ten inches, any consolidation being levelled up as it occurred.[7] Such a road could safely be taken across a bog, he claimed, without a brushwood foundation, for once laid it 'unites itself in a body like a piece of timber'. He also compared the road formation to the stones in the arch of a bridge which, once settled against one another, would support their own weight and that of any traffic. The angles of his surface stones, he claimed, united to form an impervious roof against that worst enemy of the road manager: water.

When these theories came to be publicised they were received not without scepticism, since by that time a fund of folk wisdom had accumulated and each county, even each district, had its own prescription. Some of McAdam's most vivid prose was reserved for his own countrymen,[8] particularly in respect of a tendency to pour road materials onto roads, regardless of quality, as if the expenditure would of itself cure all ills.

The surveyor, Thomas Scott of Midlothian, who reported to the Fife road committee in 1788, was advising on the preparation of selected roads and their inclusion in a turnpike bill. He was attended by a Fife land surveyor, Robert Mitchell, who was a young man at that date. Scott's recommendations on road stone have been noted above (p. 55); he also advised that a road should be not less than twenty-five feet wide, 'of which fourteen feet should be laid with metal, in the middle nine inches thick, and in the sides seven inches'.

Like Steuart of Coltness he would have preferred a road of generous width, for, he explained, 'when the roads are thirty five feet broad, a summer road may be got, which is a convenience that no turnpike road ought to want. Where there is much travelling on the stoned part of the road, however well it may be kept, it is disagreeable to travellers in dry weather: and besides, a summer road saves the mettled part, which in great droughts is loosened by the heat and blown away with the wind'.

NOTES

1. Pawson, E., *Transport and Economy: The Turnpike Roads of Eighteenth Century Britain* London (1977), 78

2. Robertson, G., *Rural Recollections* Irvine (1829), 34

3. Inglis, H.R.G. and Cowan, I., 'Maps of Early Edinburgh', *S.G.M.*, 35 (1919), 330 Map 2. The date 1759 is derived from a later publication: Cowan, W. and Boog Watson, C.B., *The Maps of Edinburgh 1544-1929* Edinburgh (1932), 36
'The Roads of Scotland: from statute labour to tolls', *S.G.M.* (1987) (in press)

5. Smiles, S., *Lives of the Engineers* London (1904), 103

6. Burt, E., *Letters from a Gentleman in the North of Scotland* 2 vols. London (1815), 281

7. McAdam, J.L., *Remarks on the Present System of Road Making* London (1822), 112, 172

8. 'Very little of the improvement [in roadbuilding technique] is finding its way into Scotland, where it is more wanted than even in this country [England], but unfortunately every country gentleman in Scotland fancies that he is a skilful roadmaker . . . A tithe of the sum at present wasted under the mistaken activity of a public-spirited gentry in Scotland . . . [would pay for them to be given a course of instruction at Bristol or London]'. J.L. McAdam, writing to Fife turnpike trustees. Minuted 4.5.1819.

The Turnpike Network in Fife

The authorisation of toll charges on the North Queensferry to Perth road in 1753 marked the first extension of the mid-Scotland turnpike system north of the Firth of Forth, and it was to be another thirty-five years before any further toll roads were introduced into Fife. As a measure to attract private capital to bring about improvements along a national highway, it was seen to be a good thing, but only the people of the western end of Fife stood to benefit appreciably from this development. Perhaps as an inducement to encourage cooperation and financial support, the Act was extended to include two other roads in that district, namely those 'to the Towns of Dumfermline, Torryburn, and Culross; and also the Road from the said Queen's Ferry, through Inverkeithing to Burntisland and Kirkcaldie' (Fig. 5.1).

The burgh of Dunfermline did divert some of its statute labour to the road to Torryburn in 1756, but even by 1780 the work had not extended beyond Crossford. The magistrates were less willing to support the road through Burntisland to Kirkcaldy, and wrote to their M.P. to say it was only wanted 'by the gentlemen in the east of Fife' for the connection it made between Dunfermline and Kinghorn. As far as Dunfermline was concerned, development of the inland route by Crossgates and Auchtertool to Kirkcaldy was preferable. Work on this was started in 1756, but it remained a statute labour road for many years.

At the northern end of the principal road, the magistrates and town council of Perth objected to the interpretation by the Great North Road trustees of the 1753 Act, in which it was stated 'that every Householder, Cottager, or Labourer, within the said Counties respectively, shall work on the Highways by himself, or another employed by him, for the Days and under the Penalties as are already prescribed by Law, in that Part of Great Britain called Scotland'. In the opinion of Perth Council, householders of royal burghs were exempted from this service. Besides, they claimed, 'merchants, lawyers and physicians . . . would make a very indifferent figure with a shovel or pick axe in their hands'. The work envisaged by the original statute labour act of 1669 was, they submitted, for 'persons enured to labour of that kind and living in the country'. There is no evidence, however,

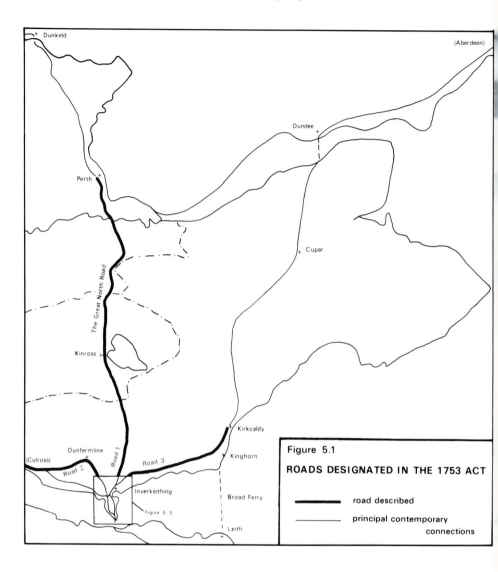

Figure 5.1

ROADS DESIGNATED IN THE 1753 ACT

road described

principal contemporary connections

that the citizens of Perth were successful in their appeal.

The first turnpike was placed at Jamestown, where a tollhouse still stands (Fig. 5.2), and the tolls were comparatively high — over twice those charged by English trusts in the 1750s. However, at that time it was the only tollbar in Fife, and for a single payment the traveller could use the thirty miles of well-maintained road between there and Perth. More than one toll had been authorised by the 1753 Act, but so anxious were the inhabitants of Inverkeithing to avoid having a toll at Bois

Fig. 5.2. Jamestown toll-house. Erected in 1756, this was the first toll encountered by travellers north of the Forth. The road over the Ferry Hills was excessively steep, and a new toll-house was built in 1772 on a road with an easier gradient further west.

Bridge to the north of the town that they paid two pounds sterling per year 'to free the town of a Tollgate'.

The road from the ferry originally climbed steeply over the Crooks of the Ferry Hills to reach Inverkeithing, but an easier route was laid out in 1769 (Fig. 5.3). New connections to the roads to Kirkcaldy and Culross were made and a new tollbar was erected in 1772.

The 1753 Turnpike Act for Fife, Kinross and Perth

In common with the customary clauses to be found in previous English and Scottish turnpike acts, there were provisions in the 1753 Act for the widening of roads and the alteration of their courses. The local people were still required to attend to give their labour under earlier statutes, although they could arrange to make monetary payments instead. Those living within three miles of a tollbar could pay an annual lump sum and be exempted from further tolls at that bar. Others who might think they could save money by taking minor side roads round a tollbar or by unhitching horses on approaching a tollbar were discouraged by fines. The thrifty traveller might be tempted to take one of the two horses of his carriage through separately (toll 4d). If the

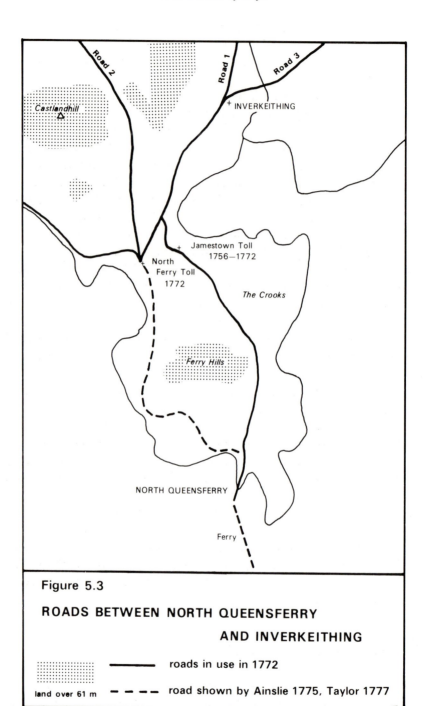

Figure 5.3

ROADS BETWEEN NORTH QUEENSFERRY

AND INVERKEITHING

land over 61 m ⋯⋯⋯ ——— roads in use in 1772

– – – – road shown by Ainslie 1775, Taylor 1777

carriage could then be drawn by one horse past the gate (6d), the saving over a two-horse carriage (1s) would then be 2d. At that time it would seemingly have been worth the inconvenience but for the 20s fine prescribed by the Act.

Although not mentioned in the account of the Fife county meeting in 1748, when the agreed policy was to concentrate resources on major roads, the burghs of Dunfermline and Inverkeithing are found to have been anxious to do whatever they could to hasten the improvement of their link to the Queen's Ferry. In 1757 a committee from Dunfermline met the turnpike trustees to determine which of the alternative ways taken by the existing route should be worked upon. In what was a singularly detailed description for the time, they recommended that the road 'should be carried straight from the Tollbar northward, through the Croft land of Inverkeithing to the Green Brae to the north, and then to be carried up the said Hill with a Beautiful Gradual Slop and a Bridge to be thrown over the Hollow Betwixt said Little hill and the Ridge Bynorth the same, on which bere [barley] is presently growing. and then the road to go thro the said Bear Ridge, which will take only a few roods of it near the Head . . . to join the piece Casway near the Whins and then to be carried towards Dunfermline all the way upon the old Road'. The bere has long been harvested and the whins cut down, but the old road past North Lodge (123823) and to the east of Castlandhill exhibits several of the features mentioned.

As the bill was being prepared for parliament in 1753, the burgh of Inverkeithing had been concerned to avoid tolls on imported iron and timber for ploughs and carts, and also on coal travelling south through the proposed tollbar, but the only exemption they could obtain through their M.P. was for 'coals carried on horses' backs for the use of the salt pans'. The manufacture of salt, the council claimed, used 12,000 to 15,000 loads of coal per year at a cost of 20d Scots per load and tolls would add half as much again. The wording of the exemption, incidentally, suggests that coal for export through the harbour could have been carried in wheeled vehicles at this time, and they would still have had to pay tolls.

The 1790 Turnpike Act for Fife

The obligation of the Fife trustees under the 1753 Act to consult with the other two counties on the two branches within Fife probably lessened their effectiveness, and it is significant that, several years later, the Act was described as having been 'very limited, being confined to the western district of the county'.[1] That the road to Perth was treated as primarily a national through route is borne out by the arguments advanced when a parliamentary bill was being sought later for the improvement of the ferry facilities. The Queen's Ferry was described as 'the principal place of passage for His Majesty's troops', and for ferrying many thousands of cattle — the service to local residents was not stressed. The Great North Road was said to branch into 'six great roads to the Northern Highlands and the North East coast'; other roads linked it with the 'many Districts of Country rapidly advancing in agricultural and commercial improvements'.[2]

As has been noted in the previous chapter, the judicious use of statute labour and its monetary equivalent had the effect of postponing the introduction of the turnpike system to Fife as a whole. When, in 1789, a bill was drafted for a number of toll roads in the rest of the county, the first roads to be listed were extended versions of the two branches of the Queensferry to Perth road, that to the west reaching Newmiln on the county boundary, and the Kirkcaldy road of the 1753 Act continuing to Crail. Unlike the roads in the previous Act, both were to be under the undisputed control of Fife trustees, leaving the Great North Road to Perth to be administered jointly by trustees from the three counties along its route.

The selection of roads, existing or planned, to be included in a forthcoming turnpike bill could provide an arena for contests of personal influence, the efforts of some sponsors being liable to prompt doubts as to their motives. In 1792 Robert Paton of Kinaldy expressed the view that future roads should be assessed by a surveyor, who would report to a committee drawn from all four districts of the county. In presenting his reasons he explained: 'The importance of a level direction to a road intended for Wheel Carriages need not be insisted upon — it is unquestionably the first and principal consideration in the construction of public High roads, and if proper attention be not paid to the fundamental circumstance, no after Labor or Expence can ever make a road commodious'.

After this unexceptionable statement, he continued: 'It must be acknowledged that the line of Direction of the greatest part, if not all of our Fife roads, has in some parts been improperly conducted, by unnecessarily passing over heights and inequalities of ground which might have been avoided, and that this radical Defect has in general

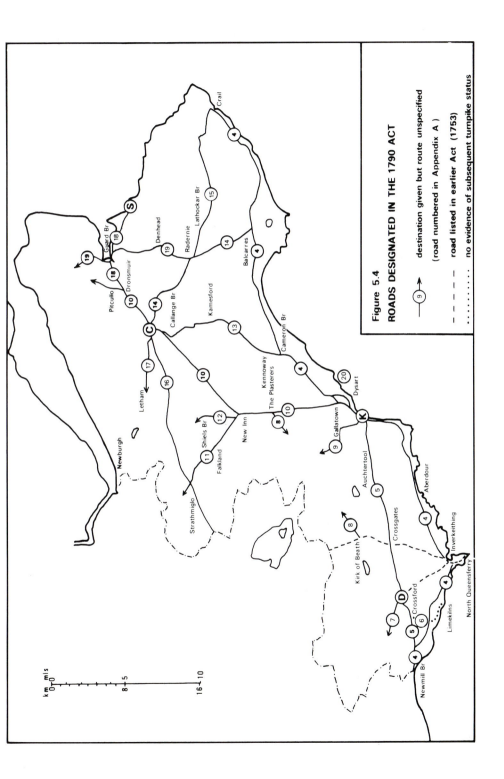

Figure 5.4

ROADS DESIGNATED IN THE 1790 ACT

destination given but route unspecified
(road numbered in Appendix A)

road listed in earlier Act (1753)

no evidence of subsequent turnpike status

proceeded from *local influence* operating in different ways:

'First, by the custom of appointing a Committee of the Trustees through whose lands and in whose neighbourhood the road happens to pass, to fix its line of direction, a practice proceeding from very benevolent motives, but, with respect to the public, the most improper that could have been devised, since its immediate tendency is to render a matter of public concern subservient to private Accommodation.

'The second mode of mismanagement in this respect has proceeded from the ascendency of particular Trustees at District Meetings, who have had influence to carry High roads out of their proper Direction over, in some instances, almost Precipices, adding both Difficulties and Distance unnecessarily to the weary Traveller or the loaded Carriage to gratify the Inhabitants of some Royal Borough or County Village'.

Paton maintained that only the county general meeting should have the power to fix or alter the line of direction of turnpike roads. Not surprisingly, the clerk recorded that the meeting 'came to no determination with respect to the said proposed resolution'.

The 1790 Turnpike Act for Fife listed seventeen roads altogether (Fig. 5.4), including several new roads not present on the map drawn by John Ainslie in 1775. In common with subsequent acts, some of the roads mentioned were no more than speculative, and their designation on paper is no guarantee that they were ever built.

Summaries of the road descriptions contained in the Act appear opposite the maps in this chapter locating their present counterparts, and from these it may be seen that for the roads numbered 7, 11, 16 and 17 (Fig. 5.4) which extend towards the county boundary there are no precise termini; however, a glance at a modern map will suggest the most probable route in each case. Road 8 can be said to have been represented by a string of awkward connecting links between other roads in 1790, and it was evidently the intention of the proposers that a new road should be built along a route yet to be selected. This is confirmed by the protracted negotiations which took place up to 1809, after which the scheme was temporarily abandoned (see Chapter 11).

As to the subsequent status of the other roads listed in the Act, there can only be one criterion by which it may be judged whether or not a road became turnpiked, and that is by finding evidence for the erection of tollbars on the road itself, or for its support from the revenue of a road of which it was a branch or extension. Table 5.1 sets out some such evidence, and this shows that one third of the roads in the Act may not have been operating as toll roads earlier than 1800.

Table 5.1

Implementation of Turnpike Acts: Evidence of Operation as Toll Roads

Enabling Act	No. in Appendix	Tollbar Installed	Remarks (S.L.R. = remained statute labour road)
1753	1	1756 Jamestown	
	2	1790 Pittencrieff	
	3	1790 Kirkcaldy (E)	
1790	4	1799 Pittenweem	Controlled by Kirkcaldy (E) Further Extension of Road 3
	5	1795 Baidlin	Western Section = Road 2
	6	1796 Crossford	
	7	1790 Rumbling Well	
	8		Not built (see Chapter 13)
	9	1791 Cluny	
	10	1790 New Inn 1791 Cupar (E)	
	11		Controlled by New Inn T.B.
	12	1790 1801 Newburgh	Controlled by New Inn T.B. New line completed
	13	1801 Struthers	
	14	1810 Sodom	Balass section complete 1804, New line Pitscottie — Radernie 1818
	15	1816 Higham	Eastern section completed 1829
	16	1804 Carslogie	
	17	1802 Letham	
	18	1791 Guard Bridge	
	19	1791	Controlled by Guard Bridge T.B.
	20	1790	Controlled by Kirkcaldy (E) T.B.
1797	21	1807 Whitehill	
	22	1813	Controlled by Windygates T.B.
	23		S.L.R.
	24		Unidentified
	25		S.L.R.
	26	1802 Rathillet	
	27/8		Unidentified
	29/31	1802 Kilmaron	
	32	1801 New Inn and Newburgh	Replaced Road 12
	33		S.L.R.
	34		Unidentified, may duplicate Road 12
	35/6		S.L.R.
	37	1807 Newport	

1802	38	1802	Controlled by Crossford T.B.
1805	39	1805	Controlled by Town Green T.B.
	40	1816 Gask	
1807	41	1809 Ferryport	
	42	1809 Shore	
	43	1810 Loans	
	44	1816	Controlled by Higham T.B.
	45	1809 Shore	
	46/7		S.L.R.
	48	1809 Argyll	
	49	1811 Teasses	
	50	1810 Elie	
	51	1810 Elie	
	52	1812 Teuchats	
	53	1811 Kellie	
	54	1845 Lochton	
	55		S.L.R.
	56	1810	Controlled by Pitscottie T.B.
	57	1817	Described as a T.P. road
1809	58	1809	Controlled by Crossgates T.B.
1810	59		Not built
	60	1810 Grantsbank	
	61		S.L.R.
	62		S.L.R.
	63	1819 Kirkton of Burntisland	
	64	1830 Blair	
	65		S.L.R.
	66		Not built
	67	1813 Pitcairlie	
	68/72		S.L.R.
1829	73	1829 Loans	
	74	1830 Beansnook	
	75	1832	Controlled by Pitcairlie T.B.
	76	1836	Controlled by Bennochy T.B.
	77	1836	Controlled by Bennochy T.B.
	78	1836	Controlled by Kirkcaldy (W) T.B.
	79	1836	Controlled by Cluny T.B.
	80	1833	Controlled by Pitscottie T.B.
	81		S.L.R.
	82	1829	Controlled by Whitehill T.B.
	83	1835 Marytown	
	84/5		S.L.R.
	86	1836	Controlled by Kirkcaldy (W) T.B.
1839	87	1840 Leven Bridge	
1842	88	1844 Kirkton of Burntisland	

Fig. 5.5. The old Kennoway to Cupar road past Scotstarvit. In the foreground is the modern road completed by 1801 (No.13). The old road runs this side of the woods on the skyline, and the tower of Scotstarvit is above the sign post.

It is known that several of the main roads in the district of Cupar had been selectively improved over a period of ten years or more under the statute labour system (Chapter 3), and that much of this work consisted of upgrading the existing road formation to support wheeled traffic. After 1790 there were also some notable realignments, of which the most striking was that easing the steep climb up Garley Bank on Road 13 just south of Cupar (Figs. 5.5 and 5.6). This completed the last section of the improved Kennoway to Cupar route on which work had begun in 1775 (p. 41).

The old road, shown in Figure 3.1, was that used by Archbishop Sharp in 1679 on his final journey. He would have turned off at Struthers onto the road to Ceres, for it was between Ceres and St Andrews that he met his death. The section between Struthers and Cupar passed the tower house of Scotstarvit, where the owner had been granted a licence by parliament in 1621 to change the line of the road from one side of his residence to the other. He was permitted 'to remove, divert and distroye that pairt of the hie streit and Commoun way quhilk lyis fra the ferrie syid to the burgh of Cowper'. Curiously, the connection between Struthers and Scotstarvit is omitted from Roy's

Fig. 5.6. Garley Bank, Cupar; The new and old roads. Scotstarvit tower is on the skyline (right). The old road followed the near edge of the slanting plantation. The new road, turnpiked in 1801, has the gentler gradient and casts a shadow on the bank.

map (1755), and this may indicate that by that time the climb up Garley Bank may have become unacceptable, the remaining section to Cupar serving only for traffic to Scotstarvit.

The change to the new line was not without its critics, and it has been noted (p. 40) that a heritor on the old road was quick to complain at the withdrawal of funds from his section near Scotstarvit. Other heritors had by 1790 enclosed many of their fields, and a road that might previously have been taken in an arbitrary line across open country had now to be carefully set out by a land surveyor after consulting the various landowners concerned. The constraints of incompatible land use were closing in.

Work on the new realignment of Road 13 (Fig. 5.4) proceeded slowly. It was sufficiently established in 1793 to be able to close the old Clatto Den road to Kennoway, and Kirkcaldy District had put up a tollbar at the southern end by 1794. Another tollbar followed at Struthers in 1801. Delays in the final completion of the road brought an outburst from Wemyss of Winthank in 1813, when he demanded that unless the last mile at the northern end was metalled immediately it ought to be closed.

One of the more enigmatic routes listed in the 1790 Act was Road 17, said to run 'by Lethem and Newburgh to the Extremity of the County of Fife, joining the County of Perth'. A map of 1789 clearly shows a road through Cunnoquhie, close to Letham, passing over Dunbog Hill to reach Lindores and Newburgh, but this latter section was hardly one

Fig. 5.7. The hill road from Cupar to Newburgh. On Ainslie's map of 1789 a road is shown from Cupar coming over the slopes of Mount Hill (with the monument), through Cunnoquhie (beyond the ruined building), and up over a col to the observer's right. A toll road corresponding to this route was included in the 1790 Act but, not surprisingly, was never built. The tower silo of Cunnoquhie Mill Farm appears in Fig. 8.5.

on which the public could be expected to pay tolls, whatever its condition (Fig. 5.7), for it was much too steep. In the event the road was taken only as far as Cunnoquhie; the Arnots Comb tollbar at the Cupar end was operating forty years later, so this section at least became a turnpike road.

Some roads to be turnpiked were reaping the benefit of improvements carried out since 1774 (Fig. 3.1), for example Road 12 over Shiels Bridge, and that part of Road 10 east of Cupar. The latter served two purposes: the replacement of the more direct but hilly route to Woodhaven through Kilmany, and the provision of part of a new route to St Andrews by Guard Bridge (Road 18). Previously loads were hauled past Chapel Well (401157) to Dairsie Bridge, and then had to climb the steep road to Strathkinness over Knock Hill (Fig. 3.5). As soon as the 1790 Act had been passed, St Andrews District received a share of the money borrowed on the anticipated receipts of Guardbridge tollbar for Road 18 and for that small part of Road 10 which lay within the district boundary.

The Roads of Fife

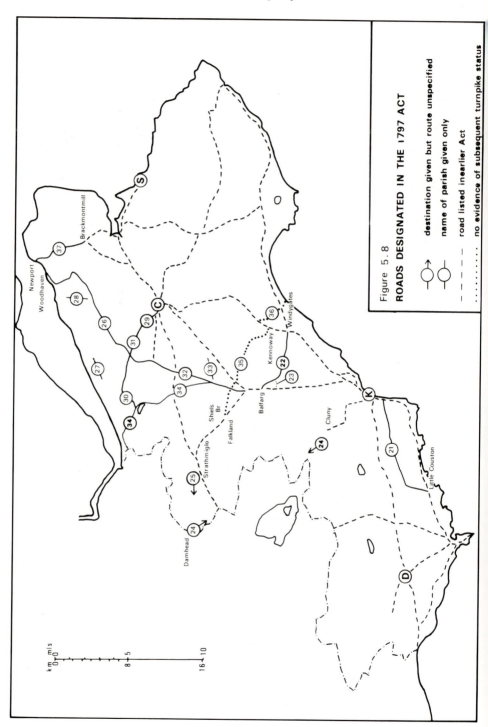

Figure 5.8

ROADS DESIGNATED IN THE 1797 ACT

The 1797 Turnpike Act

By comparison with the 1790 Act, many more of the descriptions of roads included in the Bill of 1797 were ambiguous, in that a number merely named the parishes through which the intended turnpike roads were to pass. This may have been intentional, since this would leave options open as to the exact lines to be followed. Some remained obscure and did not subsequently appear in the records as toll roads, but others can clearly be recognised, even if vaguely described.

Improvement of the long coast road from Queensferry to Crail (Road 4) was slow, hampered by lack of liaison between the three districts through which it ran. The people of Kirkcaldy were more directly interested in a more level link to North Queensferry than Road 4 could offer, and a road round the coastal hills through Little Couston had evidently caught their imagination at an early date. A line (Road 21) had been staked out in June 1790, the committee responsible being asked to make trial stretches of road 'to be able to make an equal bargain' with the contractors. Much of the road had been completed by 1793, and the need for a tollbar was being discussed a year before the Bill, which may explain why this road was the first to be mentioned.

But by far the most important of the roads to be turnpiked under the 1797 Act were those crossing the Howe of Fife from the junction near New Inn to connect with the various routes through the North Fife hills. It is worth comparing Road 32 in Figure 5.8 with its predecessor in Figure 3.1 which was the subject of preferential expenditure in the period 1774 to 1790. What had not apparently been anticipated by the promoters of the 1790 Bill was the replacement of Shiels Bridge by the new bridge at Drumtenant. The effect was to make the old road through Freuchie (Fig. 5.9) redundant. Both Road 32 and its branch through Collessie to Newburgh, Road 34, were new roads across what had been a wilderness of hummocky glacial drift, with numerous areas of marsh, and largely uncultivated. It is a tribute to the efforts of the workers on these roads that a tollbar had been erected at Rathillet by 1802. Threading its way through the low foothills towards the Tay ferries, it ran parallel to an earlier valley-side route referred to in 1723 as connecting 'the South ferry and the waterside of Dundie',[3] and which similarly passed through Lindifferon. Here the old route had crossed 'the publick road from Coupar to Perth', probably the same line as the proposed turnpike road No.17 shown in figure 5.3.

Another problem of drainage faced the builders of Roads 29 to 31,

Fig. 5.9. The 1790 Act turnpike from Kirkcaldy to Newburgh. This section, between New Inn and Freuchie (in the background), was made redundant by the new bridge and road at Drumtenant in 1804.

which lay over the col south of Moonzie Kirk and wound round the valley bottom to Dunbog and Lindores. Both owners and tenants had an interest in bringing waterlogged ground into cultivation and both wanted easier roads for wheeled vehicles. Much of the work had been done with statute labour, and in 1790 a petition, while acknowledging that access to Parbroath and beyond had been much improved by a new line of road towards Cupar, still complained that it was 'rendered in winter absolutely impassable thro' hanging spouty ground in Moonzie Parish'.

The earlier road, shown in Figure 3.1, and on Ainslie's map of 1775, kept to the valley sides, passing through the farm of Meadowside and through Glenduckie before crossing the ridge over to Newburgh. A petition to Quarter Sessions in 1831 to have it closed, presumably to prevent evasion of tolls, was subsequently withdrawn, and for much of its length the road is still in use for farm traffic. The completion of the work, marked by the erection of a tollbar at Kilmaron in 1802, constitutes the longest example in Fife of the lateral shift of a road from hillside to valley bottom.

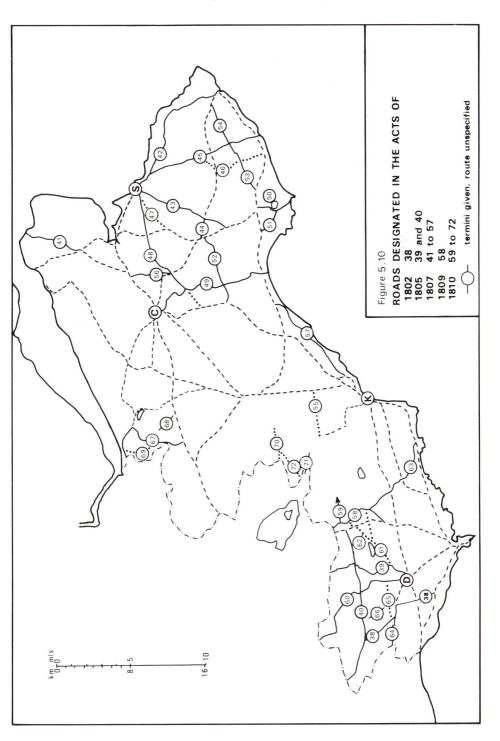

Figure 5.10

ROADS DESIGNATED IN THE ACTS OF

1802 38
1805 39 and 40
1807 41 to 57
1809 58
1810 59 to 72

termini given, route unspecified

The Turnpike Acts from 1802 to 1810

Roads authorised to charge tolls under the Acts of 1802, 1805, 1807, 1809 and 1810 are shown in Figure 5.10. Road 39 had been begun by William Adam of Blairadam in Kinross-shire in 1798 to connect Dunfermline to Kinross across part of his estate and, like Road 40, was to be operated by trustees from both counties. Nearly all the roads in the 1807 Act (Nos. 41 to 57) were in the St Andrews district and only a few changes were proposed to the existing network. Road 41 led to the eastern ferry, and had been 'much frequented by persons of all ranks', before the bridge was built over the Tay at Perth in 1771; 'but since that period', writes the minister in 1791, 'fewer people travel this way and the road has become almost deserted'. It was evidently hoped that an improvement in the road would revive the fortunes of the port.

Road 48 was new, replacing the old Bishop's Road over Magus Muir and also, west of Ceres, another ridge road to Struthers along which Archbishop Sharp would have travelled in 1679. Road 49 replaced the steep climb over White Hill towards Ceres by a route which used part of the road over Ceres Muir built in 1784, but most of which had been abandoned after the building of the new Crail road through Pitscottie (Road 14). Continuing through Ceres, it avoided the climb past Craighall shown on Roy's map and set out along the side of Teasses Hill towards Teuchats at a more gentle gradient. Tolls at Teasses tollbar (400114) were rouped in 1811.

Road 54 was almost the last turnpike to be built in Fife, not having been completed until 1844 when tenants, enraged by a proposal to erect a new tollbar, had withdrawn their labour and were finally persuaded to haul materials only in return for a special payment.

Road 57 was the first of two roads designed to link up a string of coastal settlements from Dysart to Leven. It relied upon the use of Sawmill Ford of which it was said in 1791: 'the water is often regorged with such banks of ice upon each side that there is no passage for carriages but with manifest danger. Though in summer it is almost dry, yet the water sometimes rises to such a height as not to be fordable with safety'. The writer describes a lucky escape from drowning of a farmer and his wife on horseback who were swept away downstream. Less alarming, but more constant, disadvantages were those of 'tidal delays, chilled horses and damage to goods'.

The line of the old post road to Perth, named on Roy's map (1755) provides near the Kirk of Beath another example of a direct but hilly route that was becoming unacceptable to early nineteenth-century traffic. A much easier line was selected, skirting the eastern flank of the high ground and yet avoiding where possible the peat deposits adjoining Mossmorran. Again, William Adam, through his factor James Loch, was instrumental in obtaining a parliamentary bill in 1809 for the diversion (Road 58 in Fig. 5.10).

It aroused interest, in that particular care was taken in its construction, and this was later recorded by the Great North Trust's surveyor, Robert Drysdale. In a report of 1832 he recalled, 'where the soil was of wet clay and the bottom of the road was laid in the manner of a causeway, the crevices [were] filled up with small stones and beaten hard together. The upper stratum was six inches in depth, and the stones broken to one and a half inches square'. This was a similar method to that used by Telford for a road between Carlisle and Glasgow in 1816, and described by Smiles as 'probably the finest piece of road which up to that time had been made'. Where the road could not avoid crossing peaty ground, between Crossgates and Cowdenbeath, the specification is reminiscent of the practices of Wade, Metcalf and McAdam, in that it was 'laid with brushwood; the understratum with broad flagstones above the brushwood; the crevices filled up with small stones and covered six inches deep with stones broken to six ounces and blinded'. McAdam would, however, have been content with the penultimate layer and dismissed the rest as a waste of money.

One aspect of local politics is revealed in 1809 when James Loch advises the planners of the proposed Road 8 not to extend their road further west than the new diversion of the Great North Road, since the Beath lairds wanted to use it as an excuse to have public money spent on a continuation of Road 8 across their lands, 'for no reason but because no one whatever would go that way if they could'.

Road 60 of the 1810 Act, connecting Dunfermline to the Stirling road through Rumbling Bridge, was a well-engineered road, laid out to minimal gradients and completed in the same year as the Act. It was managed by enlarging a trust created for Road 39, which now became the Outh and Nivingston Trust, and which adopted a distinctive design in milestones (Fig. 5.11).

Road 63 took the place of a road, shown by Ainslie in 1775, which ran over the Pilkham Hills and included several steep sections. The less demanding Road 63 was constructed in 1816 to 1817, the present road being further modified in 1840 by an embankment and cutting to

Fig. 5.11. Mile post on Road 60. Designed to the order of the Outh and Nivingston Trust, two of the cast-iron plates along this road lack the number of whole miles to Rumbling Bridge, which is 10½ miles from Dunfermline. See also Stephen (1967), Plate 21.

ease the worst gradients near the summit.

Road 67, which was to become a regular coach route, had a long period of gestation, having been conceived in the 1770s, as was related in Chapter 3, by the owner of Pitcairlie, with much dispute as to the most suitable line. It had been well advanced before 1790, extra carriages having been granted in 1778 and from 1784 to 1792. In 1790 twenty-five labourers from Newburgh, and the same number from Auchtermuchty, had been directed to work on this road. However, it was not completed as a turnpike road until 1813, a tollhouse at the Pitcairlie junction having been erected in that year. Its supporters claimed that it provided a valuable means of access to the lime and coal fields of southern Fife.

The 1829 Turnpike Act

The 1829 Act introduced the last major phase of turnpike development in Fife. Fourteen roads were listed, of which ten were turnpiked during

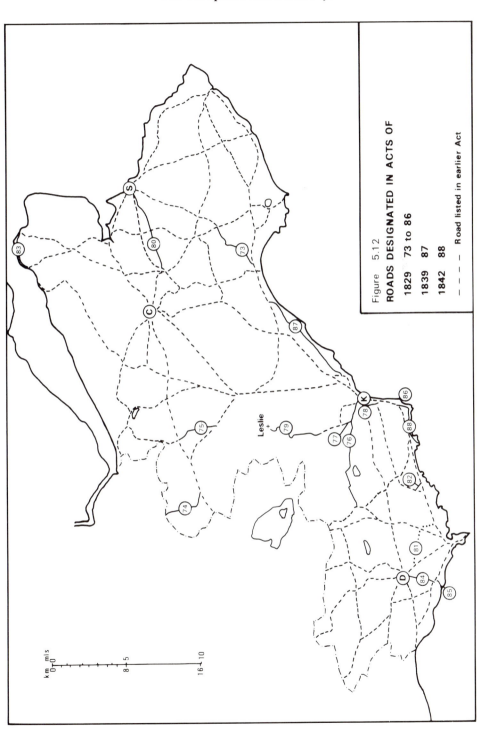

Figure 5.12
ROADS DESIGNATED IN ACTS OF

1829 73 to 86

1839 87

1842 88

– – – – Road listed in earlier Act

the next ten years. Figure 5.12 shows a scatter of supplementary links, most of which were formed from pre-existing roads, and there were two duplications, in part, of roads designated under previous acts, No. 80 including part of Road 47, and No. 87 including Road 57.

Road 74 reduced the height to which traffic had to climb from 230m (754 ft) on the Dumbarrow bank road (No.11) to 160m (525 ft); it was a completely new road and a tollbar at Beansnook had come into use by 1830. Principally of benefit to passenger coaches, the road crossed a remote piece of country past Balvaird Castle where subscriptions were not forthcoming, and supplementary funds had to be found out of burgh funds. It is said that Auchtermuchty was rendered nearly bankrupt for several years as a result of its contributions.[4]

Road 76 was of particular interest to Ferguson of Raith, who in 1812 was canvassing support for the listing as a statute labour road of this line towards Lochgelly which, he claimed, 'would open up a new field of coal and lime'. He had already diverted a road along the Lang Braes round his estate and now he succeeded in having the whole road declared a turnpike, which increased the ease with which he could distribute coal from his pits at Cluny.

Road 80 was an alternative route south of the Magus Muir ridge, which also took the carts from the lime quarries at Ladeddie and the coal from the pits south of Drumcarrow. Previously there had been a steep descent to Callange from the ridge road built by Cupar and St Andrews districts in 1785 (Fig. 3.4).

The 1839 Act for the Leven Bridge and Road

The 1839 act was principally designed to replace the unpredictable Sawmill Ford, the only alternative crossing in times of flood being by a detour upstream to Cameron Bridge. The laird of Durie had the right to ferry passengers across the Leven and he had to be persuaded to relinquish his right and became a trustee under the new Act. The road itself followed much of the earlier Road 57, but, as with several other proposed turnpike roads in Fife, there was insufficient support from the county for the venture, which they considered speculative, so that when it came to be completed in 1840, it was operated by a separate body of local trustees.[5] They incurred an initial debt of over £11,000, much of which they paid off by efficient management of the nine tollgates and with grants from the county bridges fund (Fig. 5.13).

Fig. 5.13. Leven Bridge. Built in 1840, replacing the often impassable Sawmill Ford. It was largely paid for out of tolls from the toll house (at the far end), together with eight other toll-bars on the roads leading to the bridge. Calotype by Rodger (c.1860) from *The Kingdom of Fife*.

The 1842 Act for the Low Water Pier and Road at Burntisland

The construction of the pier is referred to in Chapter 8; the fact that the consultant engineer was Thomas Telford, and that he also selected the line of the road link to Kinghorn is perhaps as near as Fife got to possessing a Telford road. This was one of the last to be built before attention, with all available funds, was transferred to the new railway development, a marked decline in toll revenues occurring as soon as the first trains began to run.

The Network in 1850

Figure 5.14 shows the full extent of the turnpike network and its relation to the first two railways, that from Burntisland to Tayport being built in 1847 and 1848, with the connection to Dunfermline from Thornton in 1848.[6] Apart from minor alterations to accommodate the railway itself and to improve access to stations, the pattern remained largely unaltered until well after the coming of the motor car.

The Roads of Fife

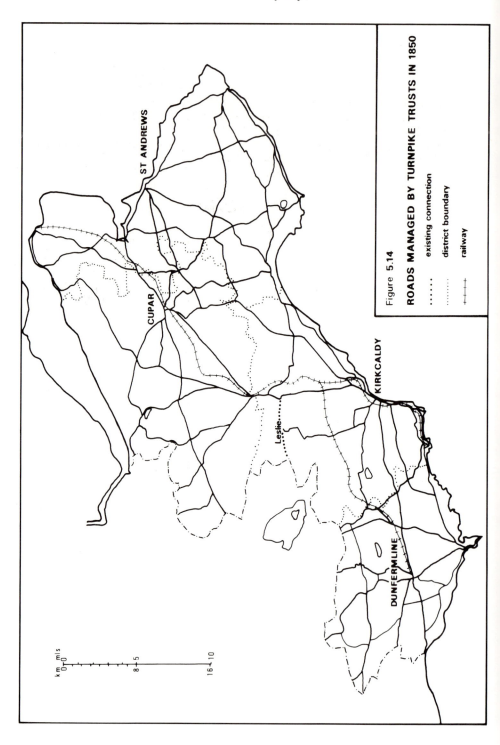

Figure 5.14

ROADS MANAGED BY TURNPIKE TRUSTS IN 1850

existing connection ......
district boundary ....
railway

NOTES

1. Thomson, J., *A General View of the Agriculture of the County of Fife* Edinburgh (1800), 282

2. Adam, W., *Letter to Rear-Admiral Adam M.P. from his father* Blairadam (1834)

3. Taylor, J., 'Description of the Parish of Monimail in Fife', in: *Macfarlane's Geographical Collections*, Mitchell, A. (ed.) Edinburgh (1906), 303

4. Turnbull, W.H., *The Story of the Lomond Vale* Cupar (1911), 38

5. Pagan, W., *Road Reform* Edinburgh (1845), 142

6. Bruce, W.S., *The Railways of Fife* Perth (1980), 58; Bennett, G.P. *The Great Road between Forth and Tay* Markinch (1983), 31-2

6
The Changing Nature of Traffic

Bulk Haulage

Just as it was the Church that was responsible for building many fine stone bridges in the sixteenth century, the ecclesiastical records kept to administer her estates provide evidence of some of the means of transport in mediaeval times.[1] The monks of Lindores Abbey in north-west Fife relied for their source of fuel on peat deposits at Monagrey, near what is now the town of Ladybank, a distance of some eight miles from the abbey (Fig. 8.3). A charter of 1302 allowed them a right of way through Collessie and across the Howe of Fife with their oxen, horses and carts (*cum suis bobus, equis, et carris*) to carry back their peats and two hundred cart loads or more of heather. The right of way (*liberum chymnachium*) must have been clearly defined, for a subsequent grant reserved the right to compensation if the monks' oxen with waggons or horses with carts (*boues, seu plaustra, equi, vel carrecte*) should trample or otherwise damage the grantor's crops on either side, *per neglenciam hominum suorum*. A carrus is believed to have been a kind of four-wheeled waggon, while the cart called a plaustrum may have derived its name from the noise made by a rotating axle, still encountered in many parts of Europe (Fig. 6.1).

The transport arrangements of another brotherhood are recorded in the records of Balmerino Abbey. In the mid-thirteenth century the monks were hauling building stone from a quarry at Nydie, west of St Andrews, for building work at the Abbey. They were granted the use of a road leading across the River Eden over a tidal ford. Permission to pasture twenty-four oxen suggests that these were the draft animals. Waggons are said to have been used, and the alternative use of sledges has been dismissed as improbable, on the grounds that it would have been impossible for them to cross the river.

No great advances seem to have been made in vehicle design over the next three or four centuries, at least in the more remote parts of Scotland, for even in 1736 little carts with solid wheels and rotating axles comprised the few wheeled vehicles seen by Captain Burt at Inverness. In the absence of iron tyres such wheels would wear unevenly and give additional justification to the name by which they

Fig. 6.1. Modern 'tumbler' cart (northern Portugal). The axle protrudes through the almost solid wheel, and emits a creak as it turns. The rung cart drawn by Burt in c.1734 has much in common. See Fenton and Stell (1984), 122.

were known — 'tumblers'. Ramsay recalls that 'carts with spoked wheels and rings of iron' were used in the early eighteenth century between certain lowland towns, but that tenants in the Carse district below Stirling were satisfied with tumblers until about 1750, and by 1763, when Ramsay was given charge of some Perthshire roads, he was disappointed that the poorer tenants could produce no better form of transport for the repair materials.

The trend towards payment of rents in cash in the late seventeenth century, coupled with a rapid growth in the number of markets, inevitably led to an increase in the amount of agricultural produce transported by road. Under the old system of payment in kind, the grain had been taken to the landlord's barns, usually in winter, by the only practicable means at that season, the packhorse.[2] Now, the farmer could sell his grain for cash and take it to market at his convenience on dry roads and in wheeled carts. For those farmers within reach of a suitable harbour, there was a ready export market for grain; by the end of the eighteenth century the ports of Kirkcaldy and Anstruther were together shipping some 3,600 tons a year.

In the north of Fife it was claimed that most exports of grain went through Newburgh, 'chiefly for the Edinburgh and Glasgow markets', but the minister of Balmerino, estimating exports at over 350 tons, stated that the port was 'the chief place on the south side of the Tay for shipping wheat and barley for the Forth and Canal' (the Forth-Clyde canal had been completed in 1790). He claimed that exports had begun in the 1760s, when merchants started buying grain from farmers in Cupar market and having them deliver it to Balmerino, remarking that before that time farmers either had to make their own arrangements to ship grain to Dundee or take it by horseback to the south coast.

Knowledge of the soil-improving properties of lime was by this time leading to a demand for coal to be carried to the limestone quarries, and transport of the product. Both minerals, of course, owed their location to the accidents of geology rather than the distribution of consumers and, in the case of Fife, there was a large area north of the Lomond Hills and their continuation into the East Neuk which was totally devoid of either coal or limestone. Apart from those places near the Tay shore where they could be imported by water, there was no alternative to extensive overland haulage.

Coal had for centuries been a product for export where it could be mined near a port, as was done by the St Clair family near Dysart, and such land carriage as was necessary could be carried out by packhorse trains. However, when the Earl of Rothes opened up coalpits at Cadham near Markinch in the 1740s, a comparison was made between the cost of packhorses and carts for the journey to Kirkcaldy harbour. It was his interest in firm roads for his coal carts that led him to play such a prominent part in the reorganisation of the road system of the county. Carts were certainly in common use by 1790 in Auchterderran parish, and the minister reported: 'There is generally a cart to every plough, and about 18 more employed in leading coal, &c. They are all two-horse carts'. A cart with large spoked wheels, recently developed and known over adjacent parts of Britain as the 'Scotch cart', could, when drawn by two horses in tandem, carry a load of one and a half tons if the road was in good condition and the slopes gentle.

If a cart of this size were loaded with ironstone it would weigh much more, and it is not surprising that in 1800 complaints were received from a contractor responsible for maintaining the road between the Balgonie ironstone quarries and Dysart, the port of shipment to Carron foundry. Possibly because of these complaints, the owner later built a private road from Balgonie to the port of West Wemyss.

Lime was normally collected by the farmers from the kilns and carried away in its burnt form, if possible in dry weather, for exposure to rain would start the slaking process by which the 'shells', as the quicklime was called, would be hydrated and give out considerable heat. Delaying the hydration until it was spread on the ground not only made it easier to distribute but also saved weight when transported. Burt in 1737 quoted a story of two highlanders who had this experience while carrying quicklime from the Borders on horses. The steam from the horses' panniers convinced them that they were on fire and the panniers were promptly cast into a nearby burn. Across the Tay from Fife, the packhorse was later considered to have been unsuitable for 'fossil and other extraneous manures', and even the transport of lime for building purposes was said to depend on the availability of good roads, implying that carts were needed.

The greater ease of loading and packing was an additional reason for trying to switch from packhorses to carts. In the case of coal, much care was taken to preserve larger pieces intact, for as 'great coal' they commanded a higher price when exported by sea.

Although representing a small proportion of the total tonnage of goods carried, linen and its raw material flax were of great local importance to the cottage weavers of northern Fife, while water-powered spinning mills on the rivers Eden and Leven consumed a large part of the 660 tons of flax recorded in 1800, much of which was imported through the ports of Newburgh and Kirkcaldy. The quantity of flax needed for Auchtermuchty alone would require 2,000 horseback loads a year. The cloth itself had to be handled with some care, and this almost certainly meant the use of wheeled vehicles. In northern Fife it provided an additional argument in favour of built roads rather than hillside tracks, and a petition in 1775 for the road over Shiels Bridge bears this out: most of the linen bought at Auchtermuchty and Strathmiglo, the petitioners claimed, was taken to the port of Newburgh, 'where great quantities of flax and yarn is weekly landed from Dundee for the use of manufacturers in the neighbourhood'. If packhorses only were needed, the existing tracks would have been more direct and reasonably adequate.

Personal Travel

It is clear from the accounts of such travellers as the Scottish laird

William Cunningham in 1674, Defoe in 1724 and Pennant in 1776, that unless one was prepared to mount a horse, mobility was very restricted and expensive, at least up to the last quarter of the eighteenth century. Prominent travellers, such as rulers or their representatives, clerics and judges, could experience the communications system through their anatomy and were among the few who could do something about it. Until the latter part of the eighteenth century, judges frequently had no option but to complete their circuits on horseback, as Dr Johnson discovered when he followed the route taken by Boswell's father, Lord Justice Auckinleck.

For those who could afford them, passenger coaches were always available, and in the seventeenth century their possession attracted the status comparable perhaps to that of a helicopter today, except that there was no guarantee that one would reach a destination any quicker than on foot. Axles and wheels were frequently broken, and Thomas Morer, visiting Scotland in 1689, observed that 'their great men often travel with coach and six, but with so much caution, that, besides their other attendance, they have a lusty running footman on each side of the coach, to manage and keep it in rough places'.[3] We know from his 'journey chairgis' that Archbishop Sharp on his visit to Fife in 1663 had the use of four coach horses, and an equal number would have been needed to haul his coach over the steep ridgeway between Kennoway and Ceres in 1679 (Fig. 1.1).

The numbers of travellers to the south swelled after the Union of 1707, when there was an inevitable increase in military personnel and parliamentary representatives crossing Fife on their way to London and back. Periods of lawlessness and insurrection in the Highlands meant the movement of large numbers of troops, but as the political climate became more stable in the latter half of the century, hitherto unrepresented categories of travellers, such as the commercial agent seeking new business opportunities, or the writer intrigued by the unfamiliar, opened up fresh economic and cultural territory.

Boswell and Johnson arrived at Kinghorn in 1773 before travelling through Fife, but well before that date there were several options open to the traveller. Visitors from the south took either the short ferry passage at Queensferry, crossing only the western part of Fife along the Great North Road, or they could choose the 'broad' ferry from Leith to Kinghorn, used by King James VI in 1617 and Archbishop Sharp in 1663, if they wanted to proceed to Dundee. So ill-defined were the roads that Sharp paid twelve Scotch shillings 'to a mane that guydit the coatch', for a road was a confusion of numerous tracks, and signposts were rare objects indeed.

At Kinghorn there were a number of horses and carriages for hire, there being seventy horses for non-agricultural use in 1793, and, as a retrospective account of 1843 confirms, 'the demand for saddle horses was so great that, in the recollection of some old men, not less than sixty belonged to Kinghorn'.

The Informers

Apart from the road between Edinburgh and Berwick, there was no officially authorised horse post in Scotland before 1655, although for military despatches Portpatrick in the south-west was chosen as a point of departure to Ireland and the postmaster was instructed to keep 'ane post bark' in readiness.[4]

Expansion of the postal service to cater for public use was permitted only reluctantly, for it was not considered wise to provide the means whereby dissident ideas could be passed with ease through the land. For most of the population, particularly in rural areas, the prime source of news was often the itinerant trader or cadger, who would visit a settlement to carry eggs and butter to market or deliver domestic goods on his return with the aid of a packhorse. Travelling between one village and the next, the cadgers were free to select their own routes without regard to the needs of wheeled traffic, and their timeless tracks are sometimes still marked on modern maps, as at Walkerton near Leslie where the 'Bloodyfoot' track can be shown to have been in use since before 1599, and was continued northwards along the Den Burn to cross the River Leven by the 'Cadgergait' (233009).[5]

Transport of public mail through Fife had begun by 1667, when authorised contractors were providing a twice-weekly service between Edinburgh and Aberdeen. The route ran from Burntisland or Kinghorn ferry to the ferry for Dundee. One runner undertook the return journey for the sum of 6s 8d, plus 1s 6d for the ferries. The connection between this single route and other parts of Fife was the subject of a scale of charges in 1711, but beyond the areas served by the few post offices, and for most rural areas in the eighteenth century, regular messengers or private servants had to be employed to carry the letters.

In 1763 the foot post to Aberdeen was replaced by horse posts in

D

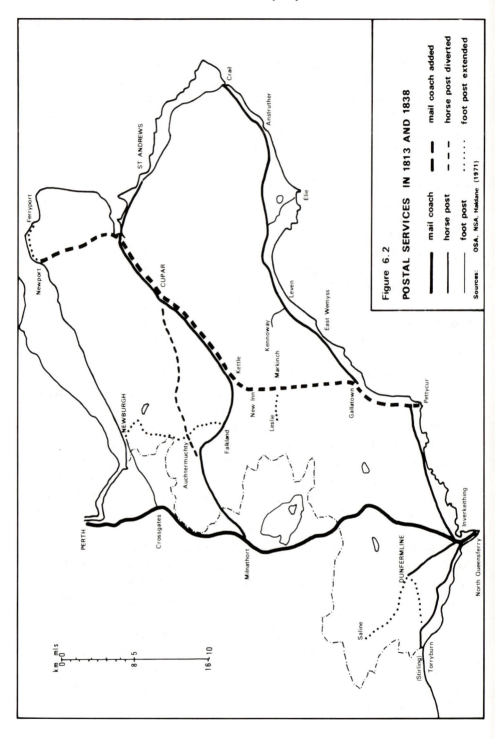

Figure 6.2

POSTAL SERVICES IN 1813 AND 1838

mail coach   mail coach added
horse post   horse post diverted
foot post   foot post extended

Sources: OSA. NSA. Haldane (1971)

relays at a frequency of five posts per week, using the Kinghorn to Dundee route, while four years later a stage-coach was carrying mail from Edinburgh to Perth using the Queensferry passage. It was not until 1771, when a new bridge was completed over the Tay, that a stage-coach continued to Aberdeen. This remained the only coach service for mail north of the Forth until 1809, and in Fife until after 1813 (Fig. 6.2). A connection at Kinross through Falkland in the direction of St Andrews had evidently been established by 1792, for the minister of Auchtermuchty argued that the post office at Falkland should be transferred to Auchtermuchty, and added: 'this is not only a more centrical place, and more business carried on, but is also in a direct line from Kinross to Cupar and St Andrews'.

The hazards facing the unfortunate postboy in winter were noted by the Cupar statute labour trustees when a petition in 1787 for a bridge at Orkie Ford complained that 'a little be-east the Freuchie, being the post road betwixt Falkland, Cupar and St Andrews, is very often impassable and exceedingly dangerous when there is any rise of water, and that the Runner has been in eminent danger of being lost over and again or else go round another way, which greatly retards his progress'. The meeting agreed to find the cost of a bridge.

One of the difficulties facing the turnpike trusts in Scotland arose from the exemption of mail-carrying vehicles from tolls. In England exemption clauses had been included in the individual turnpike acts up to 1785, when a general act for the whole of Great Britain exempted 'all Carriages of what description soever, or horses, which shall be employed in conveying the Mail or Packet'. This did not arouse great controversy at the time, but as the numbers of coaches carrying mail increased, the Scottish turnpike trusts came to realise the amount of potential revenue denied to them. Not a few ordinary stage-coach owners offered to carry mails for short distances and at low rates, solely to qualify for exemption from tolls. The trustees of Perthshire successfully contested the exemption in the case of a pre-turnpike toll on the Bridge of Earn in 1800, after a struggle lasting several years, but otherwise the Post Office stood firm. By 1812, there were two hundred mail coaches in Scotland, each weighing up to two tons with narrow wheels for high speed and capable of doing great damage to the roads.

It had been argued by the Post Office in 1798 that the limited space permitted for passengers on mail coaches enabled a few to popularise travel among those who were able to hire private chaises and thereby add to toll revenue.

After several reverses in parliament, a bill was passed in 1813, to the great rejoicing of the turnpike trustees, removing the exemption. Vehicles with more than two wheels carrying mail had to pay tolls, but two-wheeled vehicles remained exempt, provided they carried no passengers. A surcharge of a halfpenny on letters was made, intended to cover the increased cost of the tolls.[6]

The Coach Trade

Up to the end of the eighteenth century only the smaller types of passenger vehicles appear to have been in regular use in Fife. For hire, the post-chaise with its four wheels and two horses was the most popular, this being the vehicle used by Boswell and Johnson in 1773.[7] Horses could be changed at 'posts', usually inns, at regular intervals along the main or post roads. The chaise could have been a comparatively recent introduction to Scotland, since as late as 1758 a traveller to London stated that he had not encountered one until he had reached Durham. The statute labour roads which Johnson found surprisingly adequate enabled them to reach Inverness by chaise and Boswell writes: 'We might have taken a chaise to Fort Augustus; but, had we not hired horses at Inverness, we should not have found them afterwards: so we resolved to begin here to ride . . . Dr Johnson rode very well'.[8]

The coach was a larger carriage, also used for posting or travelling by stages, as a 'stage-coach', this service having been first introduced between Bath and London in 1782. Much of the mail was at that time carried illegally by unlicensed carriers, but the development by Palmer in 1784, of a superior light coach taking four passengers, returned the mail to the hands of the official contractors, who were allowed not only the standard mileage rates for the riding post but could also make a profit from the four passengers carried.

Public passenger coaches of any kind were, however, rare in the Fife of the 1790s. Kinghorn, at the terminus of the Broad Ferry, seems to have had only horses to hire, but at Kirkcaldy the minister recorded nine carriages, seven of which were post-chaises. If this had been the case in 1773, the chaise hired by Johnson and Boswell would have had to be brought from Kirkcaldy. The parish of Dunfermline had eight gentlemen's wheeled carriages of unspecified function, while Cupar boasted one coach and eight chaises.

Fig. 6.3. The New Inn. A stage coach of the 1830s runs along what is now the northbound carriageway of the A92. A second carriageway built in the 1960s required the demolition of the inn.

A memorial to the Fife trustees from the Postmaster General in 1800 pointed out that the horse post to Cupar connected with the Great North Road mail coach at Kinross and made its way 'twelve miles through a barren and uninhabitable part of the County, taking a circuit round the populous and commercial part'. Thus a letter to Cupar from Leven, a distance of ten miles, had to travel fifty miles and for three days. One solution would be a mail coach from Kinghorn to Cupar and on to the Dundee ferry, a suggestion the Fife trustees would welcome — if only the Post Office would agree to pay the appropriate tolls. They had the power to bar mail coaches meanwhile, and a similar application was refused in 1801.

While the debate on toll exemption for posts continued in London, regular coach services were beginning to appear in Fife. What is claimed to have been the first, a two-horse coach between Newport and Pettycur via Kennoway, was started in 1805, and a Mr McNab, proprietor of a hotel in Cupar, ran a four-horse coach between the same ferries in 1810, but this travelled by way of the New Inn junction (Figs. 6.3 and 6.4).

Districts varied as to whether they required compositions (lump sums) from the coach operators, in which case a prospective tacksman (tenant) was told to exclude the amount of these lump sums from his bid at the annual roup (auction) of tolls. Gallatown tollbar, north of Kirkcaldy, would levy tolls from both these coaches and they were, in

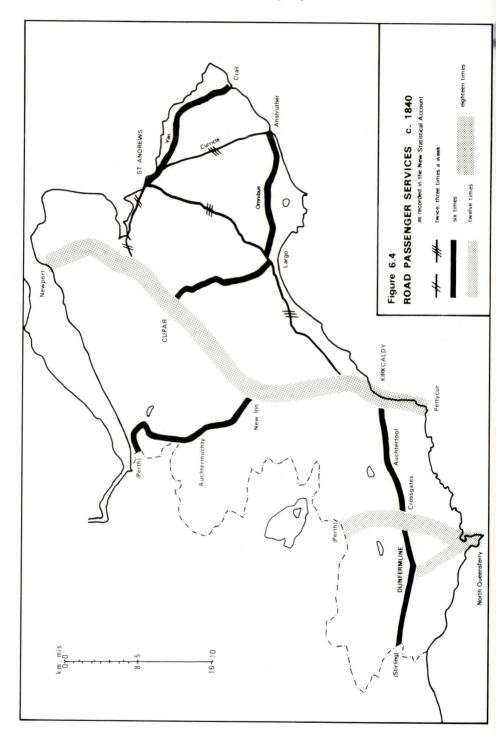

Figure 6.4
ROAD PASSENGER SERVICES c. 1840
as recorded in the New Statistical Account

twice, three times a week

six times

twelve times

eighteen times

1812, to be paid direct to the tollkeeper. At the New Inn and Cupar tollbars that year, a composition was paid to the trustees; and a discount of ten per cent was also available for a cooperative coach operator. It had the advantage for the turnpike trustees that, in return, they could insist on good behaviour to the benefit of the roads, such as the use of a screw-operated brake block when descending a steep hill, instead of the drag shoe, which locked the wheel and ploughed a furrow in the road surface.

In England there had been a great increase in the number of coaches on the roads after 1780, and the years from 1820 to 1836 are regarded as the golden age of coaching. The first regular stage-coach to arrive in Edinburgh in 1786, the so-called 'Sixty Hour Coach' after its journey time, was viewed with amazement. By 1792 it is estimated that there were twenty-two Scottish towns with connections to the capital, but north of the Forth the inauguration of such services was slower, and the period of greatest development probably corresponded to the enterprise of Ramsay and Barclay, whose 'Defiance' between 1832 and 1837 was regarded both north and south of the Border as the epitome of efficiency. It ran from Edinburgh to Aberdeen and was variously credited with a record of between twelve and fifteen hours for the journey.[9]

It might have been expected that the Post Office scheme first proposed in 1800, for putting on mail coaches from Kinghorn to the Dundee ferry, would have been put into effect as soon as tolls started to be paid by them in 1813, but this had to wait until three contractors' coaches, the 'Royal Union', the 'Kingdom of Fife' and the 'Tally Ho', were transferred from the Queensferry to Perth road, to that from Kinghorn to New Inn, in 1834. This they shared with the 'Defiance', which then proceeded to Newburgh, Perth and Aberdeen using the Pitcairlie road (No. 67 on Fig. 5.9).

The pattern of coach routes, of which reports are given between 1836 and 1845 in the New Statistical Account, is shown in Figure 6.3. A triangular area will be noted, between the Newburgh and Cupar roads from New Inn, and the Tay shore, which had no coach services. The subsequent introduction of a service west of Cupar is indicated in 1845, when the tackswoman of Balgarvie toll (Cupar) complained of a loss of tolls on the direct road to Newburgh (Road 29). Apparently, the coach had changed its route to the Kinross road (Road 16) as far as Bow of Fife and then, presumably, had returned to the original route via Letham.

From New Inn the route favoured by the coach operators was not the new road across the Howe which it had taken twenty-five years to build, and which continued through Rathillet and Kilmany. It was to be the old road through the county town of Cupar, which offered good stabling, a change of horses, and accommodation for travellers if needed. The northern road was mainly of benefit to the coal and lime carts distributing their loads to the population of northern Fife, and to the hirers of post-chaises in a hurry to catch the ferry.

The latter, together with the two-wheeled gigs, were an important source of revenue to the tollkeepers, and several claimed that their income had been reduced by people choosing to travel by the coaches, at about one third of the cost per seat and paying a smaller toll per passenger.

An even cheaper form of vehicle than the stage-coach would seem to have been offered over short distances by the horse omnibus. Enlarged stage-coaches, known as 'shillibeers', after the man who first operated them in London in 1829, were later replaced by a lighter vehicle, the 'Omnibus Carriage', which would stop for passengers' convenience on any part of the route. It was developed from a two-horse carriage used by a girls' school to take twenty-five of them at a time to meeting for worship.[10] According to the minister of Anstruther Wester, there was already an omnibus service in 1838, leaving Largo every morning.

Besides offering transport at a lower rate per mile than the coach, the omnibus also underlines a further threat to the latter's profitability, since its return was timed to meet the recently inaugurated steamboat service from Largo, and these boats brought passengers directly from Aberdeen, Montrose and Dundee to Newhaven, for Edinburgh, so that 'a journey which, less than thirty years ago occupied a whole day, or sometimes two or three, and could only be accomplished at a great expense, is now performed in two hours and a half, and for a very trifling sum'.[11]

Up to the coming of the railway the omnibus is recorded only briefly by the turnpike trustees. An application was received in 1841 from two innkeepers in Leven to run an omnibus over the new bridge to Anstruther. Although consideration was deferred, it appears they were temporarily successful, for in 1844 it was reported that an omnibus, the 'Princess Royal', licensed to carry mail, had ceased to operate two years previously. The owner was willing to have another try if the Kirkcaldy trustees would agree to a reduction in the toll, but there appears to have been no response. No doubt, the coach owners had their friends among the trustees.

William Pagan, on the other hand, was an enthusiastic campaigner for cheap popular travel, and he looked forward to an increase of 'cross public conveyances between one town and another'. Under his scheme of reform, he predicted, 'each locality will have its stage-coach, or omnibus, or fly, unless where provided with railway conveyance' when tolls were abolished. In 1843 the opening of the Glasgow to Edinburgh railway greatly increased the traffic to Perth along the road through Falkland. The trustee in charge could not keep the Falkland to Auchtermuchty section in order with the funds he was allowed; ten years later, the Cupar surveyor reported that roads near railway stations were carrying more traffic than many turnpikes.

Another source of anxiety to the coaches was the use of vans. 'A light van or waggon' was recorded in 1845 as having run for many years between Crail and St Andrews with both parcels and passengers. This clearly infuriated the coaching interests, for at Cupar in 1846 they submitted that vans, while professing to carry goods, in reality took passengers as well. They travelled as fast as the stage-coaches and at half the rate of toll.

From these and other complaints it seems that for some years before the first locomotive puffed its way over the low rise east of the Lomonds and along the high embankment towards Cupar, the best years of the coaching trade had already passed. In this highly competitive field the power of the turnpike trustees to discriminate for or against a particular form of transport could well have been a critical factor in its survival.

NOTES

1. Dowden, J. (ed.), 'The Chartulary of Lindores', Scottish History Society, 5 Edinburgh (1903), 175

2. Whyte, I., *Agriculture and Society in Seventeenth Century Scotland* Edinburgh (1979), 193

3. Brown, P.H., *Scotland before 1700 from Contemporary Documents* Edinburgh (1893), 278

4. Haldane, A.R.B., *Three Centuries of Scottish Posts* Edinburgh (1971), 13

5. Davidson, J.T., *The Road of the Bluidy Feet* Kirkcaldy (1942), 4

6. Haldane (1971), 90

7. Hill, G.B. (ed.), revised Powell, L.F., *Boswell's Life of Johnson*, 5 Oxford (1964), 56

8. Hill (1964), 131

9. Gardiner, L., *Stage-Coach to John O'Groats* London (1961), 115; Corbett, E., *An Old Coachman's Chatter* Wakefield (1974), 301

10. Roberts, E. (ed.), *Louisa, Memories of a Quaker Childhood* London (1970), 35

11. *New Statistical Account (N.S.A.)*, 625

7
Turnpike Road Management

With the exception of the Edinburgh Act in 1713, there was a lag of over forty years between the proliferation of turnpike roads in England and that in Scotland. Much of the experimental element was thus avoided in the drafting of the Scottish bills, for those responsible had time to refine the earlier acts, and to devise comprehensive clauses that covered the most common eventualities. What chiefly distinguished the acts north of the Border was the aggregation in one act of several roads. Unfortunately, this encouraged flights of fancy and led to some excessively vague and impractical proposals, many of which were never implemented.

The trustees under the acts were already well prepared to assume their duties for, unlike most of their counterparts in England, they were likely to have had direct experience of road management under a statute labour system administered by a county authority. Whatever their private motives, the trustees, to judge from the minutes of their meetings, felt obliged to be heard voicing concern for the public benefit, as often as possible.

The standard clauses inserted in successive acts catered for the common frailties of the human condition, such as dishonesty among trustees or their servants, and the more economical impulses of road users. Scottish circumstances and the nature of legal sanctions found their expression in detail. Thus, the use of the power of the judiciary in the 1713 Turnpike Act for Edinburgh was seen when lawyers' coaches were exempted from tolls and it was other road users who bore the burden of paying for street repairs.[1]

In the Act of 1753 for Perthshire, Fife and Kinross a great deal of discretion was given to those trustees placed in charge of individual sections of road, and it was easy to slip into careless handling of money. To investigate the misapplication of funds required the testimony of a credible witness on oath, after which three or more other trustees could demand payment of a fine up to twice the sum in question, with power on default to commit the offender to gaol. A 'vexatious or groundless' prosecution could, on the other hand, result in those responsible paying double the costs.

What could not be predicted was the reaction of the population to the introduction of tollbars in a new region. Those who should 'maliciously break down, pluck down, or otherwise destroy any Turnpikes, Gates, Posts, Chains, Bars, or other Work whatsoever, or the Houses erected for the use of such Turnpikes, or abuse or maltreat any of the Toll-gatherers, or shall rescue any Person in Custody' had not only to pay for the damage but also be 'publickly whipped or scourged through the Head Burgh of the County . . . upon a Market Day, between the Hours of Ten and Twelve in the Forenoon'.

A long list of exemptions in the 1753 Act is clearly designed to minimise local resentment. Materials for road and other repairs, except timber, were exempted from tolls. So were dung and lime, implements of husbandry, fodder and corn not for sale, and, by prior request from the burgh of Inverkeithing, panwood or small coal for the local saltpans (normally carried by packhorses). The raw materials and finished products of woollen and linen cloth, of particular regional importance, also enjoyed this privilege. The function of the Great North Road as a national strategic routeway is represented by exemptions of post horses carrying mail and of 'Horses of Soldiers who are upon their March, or the Carriages attending upon them'. A strong military presence was considered desirable in the aftermath of the 1745 Rebellion, and soldiers were continuing to extend the Highland road system under Wade's successor.

Little opposition to the tolls at Jamestown or North Ferry bars is recorded, but the more comprehensive Turnpike Act solely for Fife in 1790 led to the erection of many new tollbars, particularly around Dunfermline and Cupar, as is shown in figure 7.1; these affected local traffic to a greater extent than tollbars in less urban locations. When the Reverend Thomson of Markinch wrote in 1792, 'Good toll roads are doubtless highly advantageous to a country: but the advantage will be almost confined to passengers, and to those who live in the immediate neighbourhood', he was evidently thinking of the gentry rather than the smaller cultivators. He is less ambiguous in his report of 1800, when he says, 'As prejudices are commonly entertained against such practices as are new and unusual, especially if they should touch the pocket, the erection of toll-bars was, at first, unpopular, and still continues, with some, to be a cause of grumbling and complaint'.

One of the less enamoured inhabitants is recorded as assaulting the tacksman of New Inn tollbar in 1792. He avoided prosecution by the doubtful expedient of joining the army and later being sent to fight Napoleon. Another tacksman and his wife were said to have been

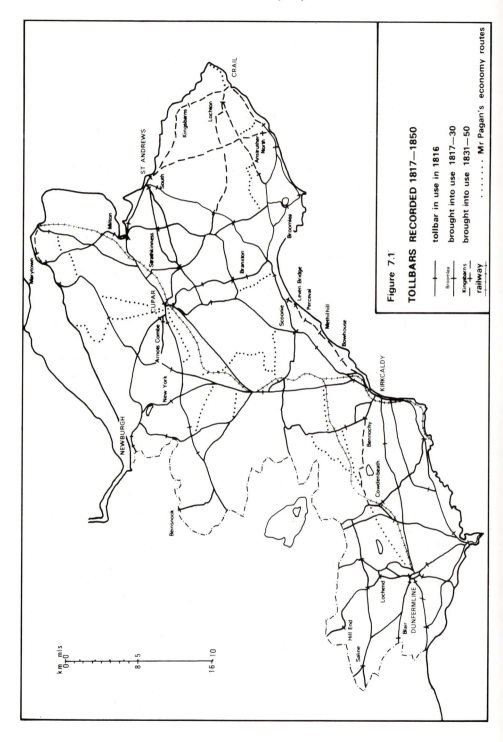

Figure 7.1

TOLLBARS RECORDED 1817—1850

	tollbar in use in 1816
	brought into use 1817—30
	brought into use 1831—50
	Mr Pagan's economy routes
	railway

'cruelly beat' at Gallatown tollbar by a local butcher, but he successfully pleaded provocation.

The people who derived the greatest benefit from the tolls were the landowners and tenant farmers for whom the cost of tolls was outweighed by the greater ease of marketing produce and resultant financial gains. It was the smallholders, particularly those on the periphery of towns, who found the tollbars troublesome, for they were constantly wanting to take their carts and livestock to and fro. The niggling disputes with tollkeepers were frequently the subjects of petitions to the district trust meetings.

It is therefore not surprising under such stress that they were tempted on occasion to commit the gravest offence under the turnpike acts, the destruction of a tollhouse or its gate. A court report in 1792 describes how a crowd collected in Gallatown, began to pelt the constables and then broke the windows of the tollhouse. On the following night, when the constables arrived to take up their positions again, a crowd attacked them and prevented them from getting to the tollhouse. The constables being thus forced to retreat, 'no person would give them shelter in any house in the village'.[2] Once they were safely out of the way, the tollhouse was completely destroyed by the crowd. By this time offenders could avoid being whipped through the town by paying a fine, but their action still required determination.

Charging the Customer

The positions of tollbars were rarely given in a turnpike act. The trustees had to consider what was the most profitable traffic and how it might be caught in what was a net with many escape routes. Decisions once made were frequently reversed, an unprofitable tollbar being moved elsewhere or abandoned altogether.

On the road out of North Queensferry, the tollbar placed at Jamestown after the 1753 Act was moved in 1776 when the road was rerouted for an easier gradient (Fig. 5.2). All the new bars set up under the 1790 Act had been chosen by a committee in 1788, with the exception of those round Dunfermline, which preferred to act independently, and at Cluny. The latter bar, a late addition to the scheme, illustrates well the divided interests of the trustee and coal owner, Ferguson of Raith, who urgently wanted to take his Cluny pit coal carts to Kirkcaldy harbour. While to turnpike this road would be to submit each load to tolls at the new bar, it was a small price to pay

Fig. 7.2. Cupar East toll-house. This stands where the road to Crail branches off from the St Andrews road. The stone pillar against the wall on the left may have been part of the turnpike barrier.

for the provision of a firm road built at public expense. The naming of Leslie as an ultimate destination in the 1790 Act was perhaps intended as a bait to the other trustees, for the road north of Cluny did not win support as a popular route to Leslie until 1829, when it was included in the turnpike act of that year (Road 79).

The 1788 committee was 'doubtful, that the road from Cupar to St Andrew's by Dairsie-bridge will not afford the expense of establishing a turnpike thereon at present', but the completion of the road to Guardbridge by the time the 1790 Act was passed justified the original plan, and a toll-bar was erected, along the road to St Andrews, beyond the more recent position of the toll on the junction with a later road to Crail (Figs. 7.2 and 7.3).

In the 1753 Act, a different schedule of tolls was given for each of the three roads. Road 1, the Great North Road, remained under the three counties' (Fife, Perth and Kinross) joint trust, but after the 1790 Act the two roads incorporated as Nos. 4 (part) and 5 (part) came under the standard schedule for Fife, the tolls being set at less than a half of those for the Great North Road. What is more, Section 18 enabled the trustees at the county meeting to reduce the rates 'without the Consent

Fig. 7.3 Cupar East toll-gates from the east. The late 19th century artist shows a broad road with wheel ruts.

of the Person or Persons who may have lent Money on the Credit of the said Tolls'. However, since the trustees themselves had a considerable financial stake in the success of the roads, they were not likely to reduce tolls unless absolutely necessary.

In one part of the standard toll schedule we see the persistence of a hoary contention that traffic should be tailored to the needs of the road, rather than the reverse. A complicated set of rules prescribed wheel widths which qualified for half tolls. Thus, a waggon pulled by eight horses or less having wheels over sixteen inches wide — in effect a surrogate road roller — could pass at half toll, provided it carried less than eight tons in summer and seven in winter.

The tolls set down by the turnpike acts were maximum rates, and the trustees had to decide what the traffic would bear, remembering that the damage it caused could be greater than the income it generated if the rate were set too low; they would also seek to set up as many tollbars as possible, so long as the expense of each did not exceed its revenue.

Many of the trustees had interests which would be injured by the cost of tolls, whether on the transport of their tenants' crops or coal from their pits or materials for manufacture. A balance had therefore to be struck, acceptable to all parties, which would assure revenue yet not tempt customers to seek roundabout routes on statute labour roads, the cost of whose upkeep would thereby be increased, or find ways of avoiding the roads altogether. Thus, when Fergus of Strathore threatened to take his carts through his own land rather than pay the full tolls, the trustees agreed to an annual composition of five pounds, and when people found they could embark their goods at the toll-free port of Balmerino, using statute labour roads, the tacksman of Woodhaven claimed his income was a hundred pounds lower.

In pleas for special concessions to coaches, it was argued that the service could not be continued unless there was some relief. Usually there was a ten per cent discount and when, in 1834, McNab of Cupar had a previous refusal reversed, the trustees justified their beneficence in granting the discount on the grounds that McNab had switched a Dundee coach from the Perth road to that through Cupar, thereby increasing their revenue.

Perhaps from humanitarian impulses or because they could not afford to be seen as wholly exploitative, there were concessions to physicians attending the sick — provided that no one shared the carriage — and for dissenter ministers to lead services in parishes other than their own. A half toll was allowed in 1846 to 'a poor women who earns a livelihood for herself and her aged infirm husband by driving parcels and light goods from Cupar to the country around in a donkey cart'.

A Multiplicity of Trusts

As with the statute labour system, however inventive the legislators in refining general procedures, the administration of the turnpike trusts was only as good as the trustees themselves; differences in style could be seen between the four districts into which Fife was divided. Cupar was the pacemaker in road organisation, while Kirkcaldy had superior resources for investment, from its wealth in coal and manufacture. St Andrews was perhaps the most rural of the districts, trustees running their affairs with a comfortable assurance and a minimum of paper work. Dunfermline stood aloof as 'the Western District', and few of its trustees bothered to attend the county meetings at Cupar or even to submit the statutory accounts, for which they were frequently censured.

Dunfermline's isolation might be explained by the fact that many of

Fig. 7.4. Kincaple toll-house. The bow-front extension gives a good view to the toll-keeper. The bar had to be placed beyond the 6-mile stone (by the seat) from Cupar East bar, to be able to demand a fresh toll from a traveller bound for St Andrews.

its most important road links were with the towns of the upper Forth and with Kinross. Several of the turnpike acts were designed to be administered in conjunction with neighbouring counties; thus the Great North Road required close cooperation with the counties of Kinross and Perthshire, and the only road in the 1802 Act entering Fife originated near Stirling and was managed by Clackmannanshire trustees. Although only one of the two roads in the 1805 Act went into Kinross, both came under Fife and Kinross trustees.

To implement the 1810 Act trustees were drawn from the four counties of Perthshire, Fife, Kinross and Clackmannan, since many of the Fife roads extended to one or other of the boundaries with those counties (Fig. 5.9); however, some lay entirely within Fife, such as Road 67 from Auchtermuchty to Newburgh. This act cites earlier acts for Fife, repealing that of 1805 and removing Road 16, from Cupar to Kinross from the 1790 Act. These roads now came under the four counties. Road 16 did not manage to attract sufficient support from Fife to pay for its improvement, and it was therefore necessary to extend eligibility for trusteeship to residents in Kinross. The other road to be placed outwith the direct management of the Fife road authority was that relying on traffic over the new Leven Bridge when it was built in 1840, and the independent Leven Bridge and Road Trust was created.

When William Pagan tried to make some sense out of the system of road management in 1845, he found sixteen trusts under Fife management and a further twelve trusts in which Kinross and other counties shared control. The tollbars in operation at this date may be seen in Figure 7.1. One effect is seen in the frequency of tolls charged round the town of Cupar, which was surrounded by thirteen tollbars. Whereas it had been laid down in the 1790 Act that no subsequent tolls could be charged within six miles of the last tollhouse passed (Fig. 7.4), this did not apply where there were separate trusts or where this provision was otherwise waived.[3]

Pagan asks us to consider the plight of 'An individual with a cart-load of wares, which he is anxious to submit to the inhabitants of the town. He enters Cupar from the south — pays there; makes his way along the Bonnygate to Carslogie toll — pays there; crosses to the next public toll on the north, and turning towards Cupar, finds himself at the Arnott's Comb toll — pays there; having a fancy to try the good people of Kilmaron Castle, which is just at his elbow, he passes Balgarvie toll — pays there; and being disposed to flee from such impositions as he thinks them, he turns his face towards the populous and thriving village of Ceres, but on leaving Cupar is caught again at the Ceres branch of the South toll, and pays there. The honest man no doubt wonders at these five toll exactions, but is counselled to stay his wrath, as altogether unavailing, because each and all of the five exactions are quite legal and fully sanctioned by the acts of Parliament.

'The Cupar South bar, first mentioned, is under the Fife Turnpike Act, Cupar district Trust; the Carslogie bar, managed well, as it should be by the Road Trustees of the four counties of Fife, Kinross, Clackmannan, and Perth, is under the Kinross-shire, &c., Road Act, [which declares] that toll is to be demanded and levied at that bar, though within six miles of any other gates; Arnott's Comb bar, Balgarvie bar, and Cupar Ceres bar, again, are all under the Fife Act, Cupar district, which has a schedule . . . appointing tolls to be demanded and levied at each of these three gates, although within six miles of each other, or of any other gates. Hence the five exactions of toll'.

Pagan's approach to the problem of paying for roads was to expose such absurdities and to search for ways in which the existing system could be improved. He pursued each argument to its limits and when this failed to convince, moved on to the question of abolishing the whole road toll system and replacing it with alternative forms of taxation.

One theme on which he expounded at length was the unfair distribution of tollbars in the county. Why was it, he asked, that farmers just outwith the tollbars of Pittenweem and Anstruther found it more economical to cart their produce all the way to the port of Crail, where there were none? Similar cases of 'circuitous driving' are also given for other parts of Fife, and Pagan obligingly suggests a route by which the thrifty traveller might go from Fife Ness to Dunfermline without paying a penny (Fig. 7.1). This was not just a mischievous conspiracy on his part to outwit the authorities, for he was himself a most responsible trustee; it was rather to demonstrate the effect of having two quasi-parallel routes, the one under turnpike trusts, the other maintained by statute labour. The traffic which paid for the road on which it travelled was being transferred to one for which it would pay a much smaller contribution or none at all.

Pagan finds great gaps in the toll system where people can use sections of turnpike roads in between tollbars, as in Stratheden, where 'both the citizens and the farmers have the free run of the turnpike roads, and freely use them. The downdraught of a toll, as the price of their traversing the roads going to mills or markets, or minerals or distilleries, never hampers their motions. Those so happily situated can have little sympathy with the toll-oppressed people in other places'.

One advantage for the trustees of letting tolls by roup was that it assured them of advance payments of revenue, free of overheads and insulated against fluctuations in the actual toll receipts. The lessees or tacksmen were often men of substance, entrepreneurs operating on a large scale. For instance, in 1791 David Brash of Kirkliston, near Edinburgh, took New Inn, Kirkcaldy East, Pittencrieff and Ladysmill tollbars. The last two were to the west and south of Dunfermline, and, perhaps because he had not inspected the situation of the recently erected Pittencrieff bar with sufficient care, he found that a large part of the traffic was evading the bar by different routes. He claimed that Dunfermline district trust should have given him greater support when barriers put up to check this practice were destroyed by local people, and he even accused some trustees of connivance.[4]

It is perhaps a measure of the tolerable state of many Scottish statute labour roads that their extensive use as an optional alternative to turnpikes was feasible, and we may recall the surprise with which Dr Johnson in 1773 reported, 'the roads are neither rough nor dirty, and it affords a southern stranger a new kind of pleasure to travel so commodiously without the interruption of toll-gates'.[5] Boswell had chosen a route which had avoided the few in existence at that time.

To make evasion of tolls impracticable it would be necessary, suggests a report on St Andrews district in 1845, to increase the number of bars to an average density of one for every two miles of turnpike road. This would require an additional hundred bars in the counties of Fife and Kinross. Pagan comments wryly: 'the very wood for the gates would cause a dearth in the timber market. It would be repugnant to the feelings of home-grown timber to be so employed. Foreign wood, and that of the most hard-hearted kind, would be required'.

Would the people submit to more tollbars, even if the county could afford the expense of building them and paying, directly or indirectly for collection? People accustomed to using a road toll-free, warned Pagan, 'abhor the idea of a tax being imposed upon it, and immediately rise in open arms against any such proposal, however equitable it may be'. Insistence on the maximum number of tollbars in South Wales had, by 1844, led to their destruction at the hands of the outraged 'Children of Rebecca', and although Pagan attributes the absence of violence on such a scale in Scotland 'to the long-suffering character of our countrymen and their commendable respect for all existing laws', he was well aware of the Gallatown incident in 1792 and referred to the fate, in 1843, of a controversial bar at Dairsie Bridge, where 'the toll-bar was several times smashed to pieces during the night, while the perpetrators . . . succeeded in eluding the well-known vigilance of the county police — a sure proof of the deep unpopularity of the measure'. Whereupon the district meeting voted for its removal. There was also a spirited response from the people of Auchtermuchty in 1830 when, on 'proclamation by tuck and drum', they gathered at a new tollbar, knocked down the pillars and 'burnt the whole to atoms'.

These were the actions of the local community, and Pagan also addresses those gentlemen who are liable to be faced with decisions about extra tollbars, and who, as travellers, value their time, and their comfort. Much is made of the 'vexatious hindrance' of finding a ticket on a cold windy night. Sleepy tollkeepers arouse his ire, as when he describes a delay of ten minutes at a toll with locked gates and a keeper who could only be aroused 'by kicking lustily at the pikeman's door'.

One sympathetic passenger suggested that the occupants might be spending their honeymoon and should be tenderly dealt with, while another, who was himself 'in bridal haste', argued that they should at any rate have the gates open to let other people get on and spend theirs. The greatest obstacle to the authorisation of additional tollbars lay in the failure of trustees to agree among themselves. In this, says Pagan, 'the interested parties are themselves the final judges, and a fair decision is not to be looked for. If self-interest be awanting, then some will be found to oppose any additions or changes, for the sake of popularity, or because the proposition did not originate with themselves but with their political adversary. Hence', he concludes wearily, 'the bad and incurable state of the toll-bar system'. To work out the system of tollbars fairly and impartially, he considers that 'the power of placing the additional gates and distributing the present ones would require to be taken out of the hands of the present bodies of trustees, and vested in neutral parties wholly unconnected with the localities to be taxed, to be appointed by some of the departments of Government'.

Unemployment

It would be unfair to see the trustees just as a collection of bickering and self-seeking individuals. They were, after all, charged with a duty to the public, which many of them took very seriously. In a society with little provision for relief from poverty, unemployment was a real hardship; wearing their other hats as commissioners of supply, and sometimes as justices of the peace, the trustees had to cope with the problems of vagrancy, poor law administration and penal institutions. Amongst the more unstable occupations was that of the weaver, who was particularly vulnerable to fluctuations of trade. Being somewhat better educated than many of his contemporaries, he could be correspondingly troublesome, as seen in the case of Auchtermuchty (p.34).

Trustees were always anxious to control wages, as one of the biggest costs of production in an economy based on muscle power. In 1801 the trustees of Cupar district, 'considering that, owing to the situation of the Country there are a number of persons out of employment, and that therefore labour could be procured at a much cheaper rate than usual, and that the laying out [of] a considerable sum on the roads for the ensuing year would be highly advantageous, both to the Community at large and to the Trust funds, by finding work [for] a number of unemployed persons at an easier rate of wages than ordinary years, they are unanimously of [the] opinion that the allocation of the funds . . . should be continued for the two ensuing years'.

The practice of employing soldiers on road works, originating in the military road-building projects under Wade and Caulfeild, continued into the nineteenth century, and could aggravate local unemployment unless action was taken, as at the same meeting in 1801: 'The Meeting, considering that the Privates of the Aberdeenshire Militia presently quartered in Cupar are allowed to go out to work which at times may be of much advantage to the Neighbourhood in which they are quartered, but as many of the Inhabitants of this District are at present out of employment and have no other means of subsistence, the Meeting recommend it to the Officer commanding the Aberdeenshire Militia not to allow the Soldiers of said Regiment to take work at present'.

The Surveyors

Meanwhile, someone had to make the best of the system as it was. The suggestion that the number of bars in the St Andrews district should be increased from nineteen to twenty-eight came not from a trustee, but from a district surveyor of some eminence: no less than the partner of that road manager par excellence, John Loudon McAdam. This man, John McConnell, was the successor of a long line of surveyors working in Fife. The first had been cartographers, such as Timothy Pont, whose patron, Scott of Scotstarvit, was instrumental in encouraging him to contribute to Blaeu's atlas, published in 1654. Another mapmaker, Gordon of Straloch near Aberdeen, and his son James were responsible for maps of Fife in the same atlas. Roy's military survey teams swept through the county towards the end of their task in 1753, and Fife was only one of several counties for which, in 1775, John Ainslie produced a detailed road map. When landowners developed an interest in enclosing open fields and laying out roads, there was a call for accurate measurement and preparation of estate plans, employing a range of skills, including those of the local schoolteacher.

Where day-to-day management of roads was concerned, the Cupar district statute labour trustee Robert Baillie was ahead of his time, at least in Fife, for in his brief office of 'director of roads' in 1788-90 he fulfilled many of the functions later associated with the professional road surveyor. At that time the most recent Fife road legislation, the 1774 Statute Labour Act, had made no express provision for the employment of surveyors as salaried staff, the trustees relying on independent consultants, such as Alexander Brown, who was engaged in 1777 to report on the condition of the roads leading from Cupar to the Dundee ferries. Robert Baillie's name first appears in the records in 1778, when he asks for the statute labour of specified farms to be applied to roads adjoining his estate at Luthrie. The 1790 Turnpike Act allowed the appointment of district surveyors, and, in the eyes of at least some trustees, made his self-created office of 'Director' or 'Surveyor General' of Fife turnpike roads unnecessary. They perhaps preferred to deal with a compliant servant rather than an uncomfortably zealous equal.

Dunfermline district refers to him by his title in 1791, but in 1792 tells the county meeting that they 'have no further use for Mr Baillie as a surveyor'. Whoever took over the job produced a notably confused and long-winded report to the county that year. Baillie was retained by Kirkcaldy district till 1793 when he resigned, to be replaced by Robert Mitchell, who could be called a professional. As a 'land-surveyor in Fife', Mitchell had attended Thomas Scott, 'surveyor of roads in Mid Lothian', when he advised the county on selecting and improving the roads to be included in the 1790 Turnpike bill. On his appointment to Kirkcaldy district, he could fairly be regarded as the first salaried surveyor in Fife, the second being David Martin, employed by Cupar district in 1799.

What probably tipped the trustees in favour of a regular appointment were the provisions in the 1797 Statute Labour Act for such staff to be employed. The new surveyor could be asked to manage all the roads of a district. Even more economical was the practice of sharing his services with an adjoining district. As McAdam has pointed out,[6] the appellation 'surveyor' could cover a great range of competence, but it is evident in Fife that by the early nineteenth century a good man could become a key figure in the successful operation of a road trust. It was he who had to engage contractors and supervise them in all weathers, measure ground and advise on laying out new roads, prepare the most meticulous reports, with distances to the nearest yard and expenditure to the farthing. He could also be asked to solicit and advertise for the vital subscriptions by which capital for new roads was obtained. The rouping of tolls and the collection of tollbar rents had to be organised; statute labour money was a particularly time-consuming item to collect, and a host of other duties combined to form an impressive workload.

While he took on tasks which until recently had been done by the trustees themselves, the surveyor was able, in his turn, to keep his masters up to the mark. Some of the reports were quite candid, where a trustee had not been taking sufficient interest or keeping proper accounts for the roads in his charge.

Not every road in a district was in the hands of a committee under a prominent local landowner. Quite commonly the surveyor would be expected to take over a road with all the responsibility for making it pay, a hazardous undertaking in some cases. After an inquiry in 1812, as to the extent of his duties, David Martin of Cupar was voted an increase in salary, and it is significant that when he died suddenly in 1822, perhaps partly through overwork, his duties were shared between three surveyors for the same total salary. Martin, it was revealed, had incurred substantial debts while managing individual roads for the trust, and although the amount is not given, there was an award from the bankruptcy court of three shillings in the pound in favour of the trust.

At about the same time a trustee, Mr Kyd, had also become bankrupt looking after the Struthers to Windygates road (Road 13), where 'expenses of management' had been working out at sixteen per cent of the revenue. Not surprisingly the Clerk remarked, 'a great want of accuracy and circumspection prevails throughout'. Add to this the information in 1830 that Kyd before his bankruptcy had run up debts of £7,400 on the Drumtenant to Woodhaven Road, and it is clear that a drastic overhaul of the administration was overdue. A new Turnpike Act for Scotland had been passed the previous year, when Hope of Rankeillour declared that he was 'satisfied that much simplicity might be introduced into the procedure of the Trust, and that all the transactions might be carried on more intelligibly and accurately, and with greater security than formerly'. The absence of a volume of minutes for several years before this statement may be more than a coincidence. It is interesting to note that a committee of the Cupar trust suggested in 1829 that the surveyor might as well take on the duties of Clerk as well as his normal duties. Happily, this was overruled.

In view of the prominent role played by the district surveyor in early nineteenth-century road management, it is curious that William Pagan, with his encyclopaedic knowledge of the administration of not only his own county roads, but also those of England, Wales, the Isle of Man and several other countries from which he draws examples, makes little reference to that profession.

NOTES

1. 'Provided always that nothing in this Act contained shall extend, or be construed to extend, to charge any person or persons riding through the said County, or going in a Coach, Chariot, or Chaise'.

2. Logue, K.J., *Popular Disturbances in Scotland, 1780-1815* Edinburgh (1979)

3. Stephen, W.M., 'Toll-houses of the greater Fife area', *Industrial Archaeology*, 4 (1967), 248-254

4. Brash had been forced by the Dunfermline trustees' behaviour, 'in not punishing those who either evaded the toll or used the Servants thereat ill', to apply for an order from the county meeting. When the district took no notice of this, he appealed to two of the trustees in their capacity as magistrates, so that they had to punish those responsible. They were, he claimed, liable to a fine of not less than 20s but got away with only a 1s fine, which some paid. One, who was a brother-in-law of a magistrate, laughed at Brash and defied him to take a farthing from him. At a district trustees' meeting Brash managed to get the whole affair recorded in the minutes, including what he thought of them.

The county had ordered four roads to be closed. Lord Elgin's factor placed posts and bars at both ends of the road to Grange and Limekilns. A six-foot ditch was dug across the coal road to Urquhart and Berrylaw. Padlocked gates were also provided on the Golfdrum road and on the road to Crossford which ran on the west side of the waggon road through Knockhouse, but the tollkeeper was expected to open them on request. Brash claimed that the first barrier had been sawn up, the ditch on the second road was filled-in almost immediately, and the Golfdrum gate had been placed incorrectly at the east end, so that feuars could not water their cattle until the tollkeeper came along with a key. To do this would have needed extra staff which, as Brash pointed out, was not provided for in the act of parliament. The district meeting however concluded that 'there being no obligation upon the Trustees to suppress the bye roads mentioned in Mr Brash's Complaint at the time he took the Tollgates, therefore there can be no claim competent to him on account of these bye roads not being suppressed, and that the Meeting refuse the claims made by him on that account but reserve full power to him to take the legal and proper steps against the persons who may have evaded the tolls or othewise attacked him'.

5. Hill, G.B. (ed.), *Boswell's Life of Johnson*, 5, Oxford (1964), 56

6. McAdam, J.L., *Remarks on the Present System of Road Making* London (1822)

8

Ways Across Fife

If we follow through the principal elements of the road pattern from that present in the early eighteenth century up to the coming of the railways, major shifts of the long-distance routes may be seen. The penetration by the firths of Forth and Tay of the belt of human settlement down the east of Scotland has dominated the pattern of communication of the county, and forced travellers to choose between an upstream diversion, to a ford or bridge, and having to cross by boat.

Armies, with their heavy equipment and bulky supplies, have historically avoided the wider water crossing, an early example being the troops of Agricola who are believed to have crossed the Forth near Stirling. As for the drovers, although we have seen that some cattle were driven across Fife between Angus and Edinburgh, most of those from the Highlands were heading for the Falkirk tryst, again crossing the Forth at Stirling.

The use, by the less encumbered, of the shortest boat passage between Edinburgh and Fife was recorded long before Queen Margaret founded the ferry service in the eleventh century, and it is suggested that a Pictish King proclaimed his triumph over the Angles on Inchgarvie, half-way across the Forth, three centuries earlier.[1]

The Broad Ferry

Except when ferry conditions were hazardous, the Queensferry passage would appeal only to those Edinburgh travellers wishing to pass through western Fife on their way to Perth. For destinations further east, the several crossing places offered by the numerous ports of southern Fife would be more convenient, in most weathers. Of these, the ports of the Broad Ferry — Aberdour, Burntisland, Kinghorn (with its outport of Pettycur) and Kirkcaldy — were those most used in the seventeenth century, while Earlsferry, reputedly named after an Earl of Fife in the twelfth century,[2] Leven and Largo later became popular crossing places to Edinburgh.

The existence of so many alternative crossings made it difficult to use the water barrier to control the spread of plague, as in an outbreak of

1584 when it was decreed that 'thair salbe no passage ower Forth be the ferry boitties at ony pairt except onlie betvix Leith and the Prettycur'; the use of the Queensferry or Burntisland routes was expressly forbidden to travellers.

In the age of sail, which of the ports at the Fife end of the Broad Ferry was chosen depended on the state of the wind and the tide. Ease of landing the graith or luggage was a consideration, for such would be carried on men's backs to the shore, as would certain passengers, such as the Countess of Rothes in 1696, whose evening arrival required that 'a man held a Lantron to sho yr Layd from ye Boot to Kinhorn'.[3]

The flexibility required by the boatmen explains the listing of all the three ports of Burntisland, Kinghorn and Kirkcaldy in the arrangements for the King's baggage in 1617. A last-minute change of landing place on Monday 19th May would have caused some confusion, for we are told the commissioners and justices of Fife had 'tane ane verie solide and goode course for the transporte of his Majesteis cariage to and fra through the schireffdome', and had listed 'the haill landis within everie parroche according to thair plewis', each ploughgate sending a horse 'with all necessair furnissing'. Either there would have to be a hasty movement along the coast or a lot of people hanging about to no purpose. One consignment of wardrobe items and luggage was given a definite pre-arranged landing place, at Kirkcaldy on 15th May, requiring eighty carts for its conveyance.

The Overland Routes

We can only speculate as to the route taken by the King and his considerable retinue between landing in Fife and reaching Falkland. There could be no practicable alternative, however, to the way over the Markinch col, unless it was along one of the ancient tracks across the eastern shoulder of the Lomonds near Balfarg. Similarly, the scarp-foot route through Cupar and thence over the hills to Dundee waterside would offer few alternatives. As to his return from Perth between the 7th and 9th of July, the route may be identified from the following sections of road named as in need of repair: 'betuix the burne of Cragye and the calsay benorthe the brig Erne'; 'fra the eist end of Shillis Brig be eist the brig of Erne, to the mid burne in the glane of Abernethie that rinnis besouth Monquhirrit'; and 'fra the said mid burne to Falkland'. A route known locally as 'The King's Road' can still be traced over the Dumbarrow col and down into Strathmiglo.

Archbishop Sharp in 1663, from his accounts, also seems to have used the Markinch col route to reach Falkland. Landing at Kinghorn, he paid for 'a bagage horse hyre that turned frome Balfarg', and he also travelled through Cupar.

Use of the Broad Ferry as the main entry for Fife from Edinburgh is confirmed in the early eighteenth century by Sibbald, who names Pettycur as the 'harbour for passage boats'. A subsequent editor notes that about 1763 it was 'greatly improved and enlarged', but was subject to silting up. From the earliest maps to show any roads at all it is evident that the Broad Ferry was regarded as an alternative means of getting to Perth, using one of the routes which skirted the west side of the Lomonds and crossed Glen Farg. A tolerably accurate map by Dorret in 1750 shows a road as running from Kinghorn through Scotlandswell and along the east shore of Loch Leven, and the map from Roy's survey at about the same time shows the road starting from Burntisland and passing east of Lochgelly to join the same route (Figs. 1.4 and 2.3).

After the period of road improvement in the 1750s when the Great North Road was turnpiked, the eastern route to Perth was evidently abandoned, for it does not appear on the Ainslie map of 1775. Its attempted revival was the subject of petitions by coal owners near Ballingry in 1836 who would have found an old road made up at public expense very useful. But the investigating committee concluded that the old Kinghorn to Perth road by Capledrae 'could not be adapted for wheel carriages'. A new road link had indeed been built between Burntisland and the diverted section of the Great North Road at Cowdenbeath (Roads 63 and 58), an improvement of the old White Rashes road across Mossmorran, so that there was really no case for the old road, which was allowed to become almost unrecognisable.

The road north from the ferries through Kirkcaldy was evidently carrying heavy traffic in 1730, when there were petitions asking for it to to be causewayed at Pathhead. From there to Gallatown the road corresponded to the line along which the main seam of coal mined at Dysart could be followed inland. John Ainslie's map shows a row of coal pits along the road, and it could be its additional function as a coal road which made this, rather than one of the number of parallel roads going north, the preferred line for improvement.

At Gallatown the question of whether to take the road to Cupar by going north through the Markinch gap, or north-east over the 'rigging'

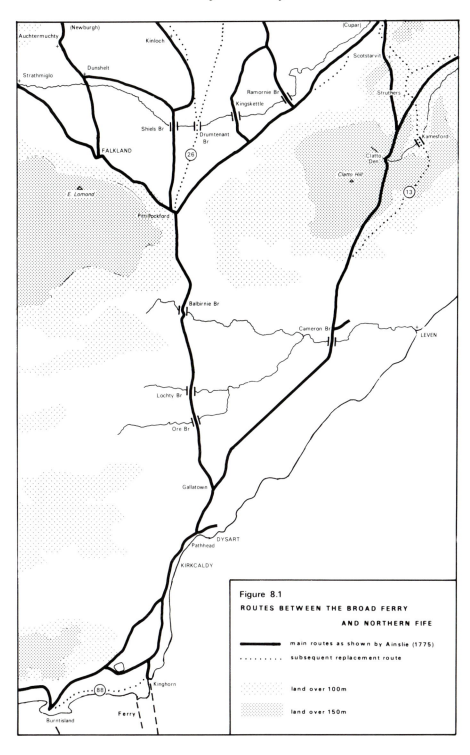

Figure 8.1

ROUTES BETWEEN THE BROAD FERRY

AND NORTHERN FIFE

main routes as shown by Ainslie (1775)

subsequent replacement route

land over 100m

land over 150m

Fig. 8.2. Collessie and the hill road to Lindores. The monks of Lindores Abbey were permitted by a 14th-century charter to fetch peats from south of the village. The track shown by a dotted line would have been a suitable route.

by Kennoway depended upon the load to be carried (Fig. 8.1). From the second branched off the road to St Andrews, and it was from Kennoway that Archbishop Sharp had set out to travel to that city before he was murdered in 1679. The road led across a sparsely populated upland area, exposed in winter and with several natural hazards, such as the awkward descent into Clatto Den. The northern part of the road into Cupar was joined by one from Leven, and it is notable that when in 1621 Scotstarvit was granted a licence 'to remove, divert and distroye' a road passing the tower house, it was described as 'that pairt of the hie streit and Commoun way quilk lyis fra the ferrie syid to the burgh of Cowper', for in good weather a ferry from Leven would have been an easier way to Leith and Edinburgh than by the longer road to Kinghorn.

For heavy loads the road over the low col at Pittillockford offered the best route to Cupar, and indeed across the whole peninsula, at least up to the end of the eighteenth century, for a string of villages had existed for centuries along its course, while the sandy heaths and marshes of the Howe to the north were of little agricultural value and considered fit only to grow trees. In the section between Gallatown and Pittillockford fine stone bridges had been provided across the Ore and

Fig. 8.3. Collessie from the hill track to Lindores. To the right of Collessie church tower can be seen the spire of the church in modern Ladybank. It was near the latter that the monks are believed to have dug their peats.

the Lochty at an early date, and by 1725 a laird from Markinch was able to describe The Plasterers, south of Balbirnie, as 'a very convenient inn, built by the best plaisterer there ever was in Scotland'.[4] He also notes an inn at Paddockhall further north, but this was soon to be superseded by an establishment which stood at what might be called the hub of the Fife road system, the New Inn (Fig. 6.3), a name later given to the most lucrative of the tollbars, a short distance to the south. The old term of Pittillockford (Fig. 8.1) fell into disuse thereafter in the road authority's records.

If the most popular route from New Inn to Dundee was through Cupar, it was always possible to take one of the tracks from among the somewhat confused network of routes created by travellers across the Howe on their way to northern Fife. The most direct way lay over the Eden at Shiels Bridge, but the traveller could pass some way along the Cupar road and branch off across the bridges at Kettle or Ramornie. Having reached the slopes carrying the villages of Collessie, Monimail and Letham, one could choose a hillside road, such as that used by the monks of Lindores Abbey (Figs. 8.2 and 8.3), to reach Newburgh, or attain the same destination through Monimail and Whitehill or Letham

Fig. 8.4. A superior 14th-century cart. Hilly routes could be managed, given sufficient equine determination and the odd human shoulder to the wheel.

and Dunbog. If it was desired to use the Dundee ferry, there was the road to Luthrie by way of Letham and Cantyhall.

The programme of improvement that resulted in the building of Drumtenant Bridge and the new roads from New Inn to Collessie and to Melville Gates caused many of the roads on Ainslie's map to fall into disuse. As with the valley-bottom road which now led to Lindores, the whole success of these improvements depended on the draining of the winding depressions that separated the North Fife hills. Lindifferon ceased to be the crossroads between traffic to Dundee from Kinghorn and to Newburgh from Cupar that was described in 1723.[5]

The Tay Ferries

A wide range of routes was open to the traveller between Stratheden and Dundee (Fig. 8.6). There was the hill route from Luthrie through Hazleton Walls and Gauldry, daunting to anyone with a heavy load, and a similar problem was presented by a journey from Cupar directly north through Kilmany. The search for the best way round the ridge on which Gauldry stands engaged the attention of the Cupar and St Andrews road trustees for many years before one was chosen. Although there is evidence that the route through Balmullo had been earmarked for development in the 1770s or earlier, the road north of Kilmany was used all through the eighteenth century, and a deep hollow way east of Round Hill bears witness to the volume of traffic carried. At the time

Fig. 8.5. Valley routes through the North Fife hills. Viewed from an old hill road (No. 17 of the 1790 Act), Mount Hill is to the right (see also Fig. 5.7). The road from New Inn constructed in the 1730s sweeps round to the cross-roads near Parbroath. The old valleyside route to Newburgh can be seen as a hedge line to the left of Parbroath, with the modern bottom road running parallel.

of Roy's survey the way led through Black Wood and down the north flank of Newton Hill, crossing the jumble of glacial debris in the Wormit valley to climb up Flass Bank and down into Woodhaven. Twenty-five years later, Ainslie showed the road, still in use, which passes east of Gauldry and winds down through Peasehill farm to the same ferry.

Woodhaven, while seemingly the foremost passenger ferry port up to 1800, was only one of several active ports on the Fife shore of the lower Tay. At Balmerino the minister recalled in 1791 that 'coal and lime are brought . . . in such quantities as to serve all the purposes of fuel and agriculture'. The relative cheapness of water transport meant that lime could be imported to northern Fife from Lord Elgin's works at Charlestown or even from England more economically at that time than by the existing road from the Forthar quarry near New Inn.[6] We are told that since about 1760 Balmerino had become a major outlet for wheat and barley destined for the Forth area. 'Before that period', notes the minister, 'the farmers carried their victual either to Dundee, where the merchants shipped the surplus, or transported it upon

E

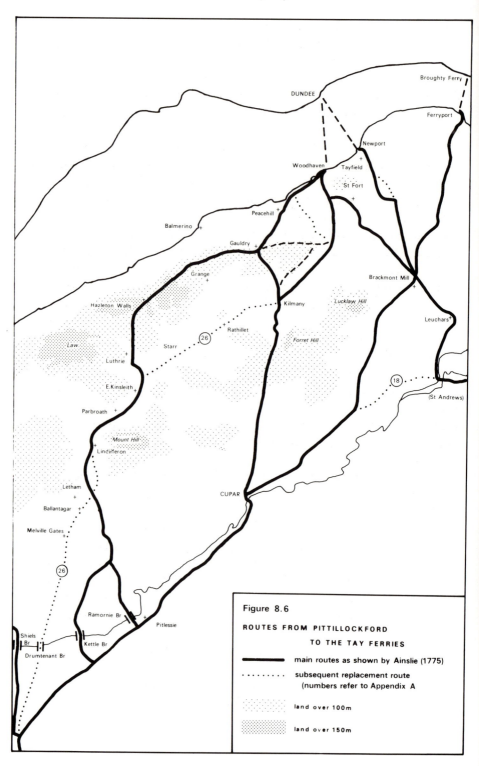

Figure 8.6

ROUTES FROM PITTILLOCKFORD

TO THE TAY FERRIES

━━━━━━ main routes as shown by Ainslie (1775)

· · · · · · · · subsequent replacement route
(numbers refer to Appendix A

land over 100m

land over 150m

horseback to the south coast'. When tolls were introduced, Balmerino had the advantage of being toll-free, and was used as an example of legitimate toll avoidance by William Pagan, since it attracted some of the traffic which would otherwise have gone to Woodhaven. It is doubtful, however, with the restricted landing facilities, whether it could ever have been a serious competitor to Woodhaven as a passenger ferry.

At the eastern end of the shore Ferryport-on-Craig (to be renamed Tayport after the building of the railway) is recorded in an Act of 1474 which sets out the charges to be made at ferries: 'And at the Port-in-Craige, ane penny for the man, and the horse ane penny: And quhat ferriers that dois in the contrarie, sall pay fourty shillings to the King, and his person prisoned at the will of the King'.[7] The ferrymen were also required to 'make brigges to their boates' because there was no fixed landing stage. Indeed, in 1790 it was customary to draw up vessels to the point of a craig for easier embarkation of horses, by which the minister explains the name of the port. He blames the building of a bridge at Perth in 1771 for a subsequent reduction in traffic which, he says, caused the road to the ferry to become 'almost deserted'. 'The drovers, however, frequently pass here, having good conveniency for their cattle on both sides of the river'. With such mixed company, the prospects as a passenger port would seem to have been limited. Only the improvement of the Cupar to Brackmontmill road made it a realistic option for passengers from the south, and then only if they were bound for Aberdeen, through Broughty Ferry, rather than Dundee.

The supposed supremacy of Woodhaven towards the end of the eighteenth century can be based on its selection as a terminus on the road shown by Dorret (1750), and also by Ainslie (1775). It is the port referred to as the destination of several routes in the Cupar district which were being improved. The original line of the new turnpike built in 1790 ran, as Ainslie shows, across the Wormit valley and passed over the ridge between Wormit Hill and St Fort Hill. In 1792 Stuart of St Fort expressed concern about the steepness of the section descending the north slope into Woodhaven; with the support of the St Andrews district trustees an improvement was made in the line and by 1794 a map showed an additional road winding down to the port, with an easier gradient.

By 1804, however, Stuart was instrumental in having a new turnpike road built on the west side of the Wormit valley, along the line of the

Fig. 8.7. Flass Bank from the Newton Hill road. The road in the foreground is that shown by Roy in 1755, and leads over the ridge on the left. Beyond the sandpits a road came in from St. Andrews past St Fort house (now demolished) to meet the first road on the skyline.

present B946, which passed round Wormit Hill. He made a connection to the new road from Baronsloan (419251) as part of an arrangement to close the old road over the ridge. In a later court case over a right of way it was revealed that Stuart had objected to a road from St Andrews which, before joining the old road, 'went very close on the south side of the House of St Fort, and certainly was not very agreeable to the family residing there'. As an additional argument he had added, 'Besides it was very inconvenient for the Public from their having to go up one steep hill and down another, of which those who had occasion to travel on it or to drive loaded carriages had frequent cause to complain' (Fig. 8.7).

The improvement was welcomed by travellers if the tacksman of Cupar East tollbar is to be believed, for later in 1804 he asked for a reduction in rent on the grounds that 'the new road from New Inn was more used than that going through Cupar'. The road from New Inn was Road 26 through Kilmany and thence to Woodhaven on Stuart's new road, while the Cupar traffic which had formerly used the steep route through Gauldry now went through Brackmontmill (near St

Michael's). Support for the Brackmontmill road had not been unanimous among the Cupar trustees. Some considered it would be too expensive and claimed that the Kilmany road was adequate. They also added the criticism that the road would be going 'out of the most populous part of the country', claiming that this was contrary to the spirit of the 1790 Turnpike Act. The fickleness of traffic in switching from one road to another brought benefits to Mr Stuart in this case, but the ferry he owned at Woodhaven was vulnerable to competition from another, further downstream, at Newport. The Newport ferry had been founded comparatively late, by the Guildry (traders' association) of Dundee, in 1713, and it was due to the enterprise of the owner, William Berry of Tayfield, that it began to draw traffic away from Woodhaven in the early 1800s. Travellers from Cupar had become accustomed to using the lower road through Brackmontmill (St Michael's) and could now equally well go from there to Newport.

Berry wanted a new road to his pier, and in 1799 he asked the surveyor, Robert Mitchell, who had advised the trustees on the 1790 Act, to prepare a scheme for presentation to St Andrews district. Stuart had different ideas and sought to persuade the trustees by arranging independent surveys, one by a local schoolmaster. These were viewed with disfavour by Mitchell, who wrote to Berry, 'If Mr Stuart, or those who are advocates for these alterations, would honestly say that they want the road to go where it is most convenient for their purpose of inclosing, or to please their whim, this would be telling truth and they would get credit for it. But to pretend that they are serving the public by such an alteration is insulting common sense'.

The next year Berry managed to convince the St Andrews trustees that Mitchell's route was the most suitable, but it was not until Berry had made a mile of the road on his own land and written to several other trustees that he was finally able to get their support for the spending of public funds. The time had come to consider shifting the principal ferry port eastwards, towards the mouth of the Tay, on the grounds of public safety alone. The crossing from Woodhaven was not an easy passage and, in the words of Captain Basil Hall, an expert witness in a later investigation, 'owing to the strong tides, the numerous shoals in the river, and the frequency of hard gales, so much risk and inconvenience generally attended the passage, that many people preferred the circuitous route of Perth to this short but dangerous and inconvenient ferry'.

At a county meeting in 1804 Berry marshalled a number of

Fig. 8.8. Pack house at Woodhaven. The passenger ferry was discontinued in 1805, in face of competition from Newport (seen along the shore), but the quay remained a place for handling merchandise. The pack house was rebuilt in 1799, the date on the plaque.

arguments in favour of the change to Newport: it was opposite and one mile nearer to Dundee than was Woodhaven; the water was deeper, with fewer sandbanks opposite the pier, the boatmen having to go eastwards from Woodhaven to clear the shoals at low water; he had the backing of the Post Office who had expressed a preference for Newport; and lastly, Newport had recently become increasingly popular as a port for shipping grain and for unloading coal and lime. Berry pointed out that the two ferries could be to some extent complementary. A road joining them would give the traveller a last-minute choice where wind and tide were critical factors, and both were roughly equidistant from the St Michael's junction. There was also the consideration that all three ferries — Woodhaven, Newport and Ferryport-on-Craig — were in need of improvement, and where public money was involved it would be better to spend it on the most promising terminal.

By the following May an independent committee, despite the assertion that 'means had been used to prejudice some of the members . . . against it', came out in favour of Newport, adding the additional points that the road to Woodhaven had fallen into disrepair, and that

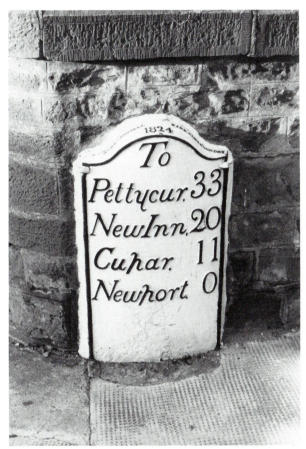

Fig. 8.9. Mile 'stone' at Newport ferry. These fine products of the Kirkcaldy foundry were erected all along the Great Road through Fife.

the boatmen had become disheartened and were giving up the service.

An amicable compromise was eventually reached between the two ferry owners whereby the tolls from the bars on the approach roads were pooled and used to pay off the road debts. Woodhaven continued to be used to a diminishing extent as a ferry port. What brought about its demise in this capacity was not so much Berry's energetic promotion of the rival ferry as a greater concern for safety and a demand for larger but fewer vessels. In 1807 a total of twenty-five boats served the two ferries, manned by a hundred men and boys, which 'were found to be alike unsuitable for the safety and accommodation of the public', a concern which was to be justified in 1815 when seventeen lives were lost in an accident. The number of boats was promptly reduced, piers and landing places were improved, and in 1819 the ferries were placed under a statutory trust. When the sailing vessels came to be replaced by a steamboat in 1821, this at first plied alternately to Woodhaven and to Newport, but after a year Woodhaven was omitted and thereafter became restricted to goods traffic.

The effect on Ferryport was similar. The minister in 1836, while following his predecessor in blaming the reduced fortunes of the port on a bridge at Perth, also claimed that 'neither horses nor cattle . . . cross the river by this passage since the erection of the steam boat between Newport and Dundee'. The passage still had 'to be effected in every state of the weather by small sailing boats', and he adds, 'scarcely anywhere else in the kingdom is this now the case on a passage of nearly two miles. A steam boat is therefore much desiderated'.

Improving the Broad Ferry

The road connections to and from the ferries at the southern end of the Great Road through Fife were briefly noted at the beginning of the chapter from the point of view of a late eighteenth-century traveller. He was most likely to be put ashore at Pettycur (Fig. 8.10), and this was to remain the case for subsequent travellers up to 1845, when the improvements to Burntisland harbour were completed. When contrasted with the wide range of alternative approach roads to the Tay ferries across the whole of northern Fife, those to the Broad Ferry were more restricted. On arrival at one of the three main ports there was no practical alternative to passing through the one long street of Kirkcaldy, described in 1795 as 'winding and irregular, deformed by the frequent projection of contiguous houses and stairs, and, as the traveller daily feels, wretchedly paved'. Associated with these ports was Aberdour, which shared the same terminals on the Edinburgh side — Leith, Granton and Newhaven — but Aberdour never handled more than a small fraction of the total passengers, and in 1790 it was stated that there was but one ferry boat to Leith 'principally employed in carrying grain'.

Whatever the weather, Burntisland had certain natural advantages, and even in 1710 Sibbald noted that there was 'a large and safe harbour, for ships of the biggest size; there may be docks here, and at the east end of the town. Because of its situation and accommodation for landing and for the entertainment of passengers, it is one of the

Fig. 8.10. Pettycur from Grange Hill. The small promontory carries the quay at which passengers landed from Leith. The harbour remained usable only so long as it was kept clear of sand, and this ceased when trains started to run from Burntisland in 1847. The boulder on the left emphasises the danger of rock falls; the area of ground built up to take the new road, and later the railway, can be seen.

three towns for passage over the firth, and well frequented'. The minister in 1791 is also eloquent in its support, and claims the harbour is 'one of the best in Scotland'. He advocates its development as a naval base, and hopes that should Burntisland become the principal ferry port to Leith or Newhaven the streets, which he claims were last repaired as part of a bargain with Oliver Cromwell, might at last receive some attention.

His fellow minister at Kinghorn takes a less sanguine view, says little about improving the streets, and is ambivalent about the ferry, which he suggests 'may justly be considered as having been hitherto the ruin of Kinghorn, both in respect of industry and morals'. He recognises the economic benefits, but as a spiritual guardian deplores the effect on public behaviour of 'all the banditti and vagabonds of the country continually passing and repassing through this great thoroughfare, and occasionally stopping and lodging for days and weeks together'. He has, however, some praise for the watermen to whose skill and sobriety he attributes their good safety record, so that 'there is not an instance of so much as one of these boats having been lost within the memory of man'.

The lack of good road communication between Burntisland and Kinghorn was perhaps the chief reason why the former was always secondary as a ferry port to Pettycur; the only road up to 1840 was by way of Kinghorn Loch, with a steep bank to climb. It was evidently in poor condition in 1800 after it been 'much trafect in wet seasons, owing to the herring taken at Burntisland', and was presumably not suitable for carrying heavy wheeled vehicles. There was an alternative line, shown by Roy, requiring an arduous climb up to Grange Hill and running along the exposed clifftop north of the Bents (257865), where Alexander III is reputed to have been killed when thrown from his horse in 1286. Ainslie shows no clifftop road, but only a truncated track leading towards Pettycur along the shore, which suggests there was a means of communication with Kinghorn at low tide.

The need for a proper road was certainly recognised in the turnpike acts, that of 1753 including 'the Road from the (said) Queen's Ferry through Inverkeithing to Burntisland and Kirkcaldie'. It was again incorporated in the longer road at the beginning of the 1790 Act which led to Crail through Inverkeithing, Aberdour and Kirkcaldy (Road 4). The first road of the next turnpike act in 1797 (Road 21) joins that from Aberdour to Kirkcaldy by an inland route avoiding Burntisland and was known as 'the road to Queensferry by Kilrie'.

The trustees were clearly more eager to improve communications with Queensferry and West Fife than they were to develop Burntisland at this stage, but the next fifty years were to see a number of proposals to have the Broad Ferry recognised as a national asset and to persuade the government to invest in improved piers. In 1807 Rennie made a survey of Pettycur but concluded that Burntisland was the more suitable port, although he did point out the difficulty of access along the hilly road past Kinghorn Loch.

A new urgency was added to the question of ferry terminal improvement in 1818 when Kirkcaldy introduced a steamboat. There had been rivalry between Kirkcaldy and Kinghorn over ferry rights since the seventeenth century, and this had not been diminished when ferry trustees were appointed under an act of 1792. Further steamboats were now acquired and the schedule of calls included Aberdour, covering some twelve miles of coast. Attempts by a local entrepreneur, Thomas Greenhill, to take over the ferries resulted in financial disaster, the construction of new piers being beyond his resources; having 'admitted the rashness and precipitancy of his conduct', he withdrew from the enterprise in 1826. Although the principles he was working on were admirable, the failure resulted in a delay of several years before a single crossing place for the Broad Ferry was again considered.

A fresh scheme, providing for a low-water pier at Burntisland, was put forward by the Duke of Buccleuch and Sir John Gladstone backed by the Act of Parliament in 1842 (summarised in Chapter 5). Three boats were purchased in 1844, in the same year that the Edinburgh and Northern Railway Company was formed. They bought ground for the railway in 1845 and also the harbours of Kinghorn and Pettycur. By the time the first train ran from Burntisland to Cupar in 1847, they had bought up and extinguished the ferry rights; regular scouring of Pettycur ceased, removing any possibility of competition since the old harbour rapidly silted up and became virtually useless for passage boats.

Access to Burntisland from Kinghorn was greatly improved by a new road specified in the 1842 Act (Road 88), undertaken by the turnpike trustees of Kirkcaldy district. In 1843 their road manager, Mr McConnell, surveyed the line of the new road, to be built up by material excavated from the steep cliffs, and it was completed in September 1844. Attempts by the trustees to erect a tollbar on the road aroused fierce opposition from the burgh which was supported by the county meeting and, after a brief period, the bar was removed and the road remained toll-free.

NOTES

1. Dean, P. and C., *Passage of Time* North Queensferry (1981), 2
2. Graham, A., 'Archaeological Notes on some Harbours in Eastern Scotland', *P.S.A.S.*, 101 (1968-9), 200-85
3. Bodie, W.G.R., 'Introduction to the Rothes Papers', *P.S.A.S.*, 110 (1978-80), 408
4. Mitchell, A. (ed.), 'Macfarlane's Geographical Collections Vol. 1', *Scottish History Society*, 51 (1906), 300
5. Mitchell (1906), 303
6. Bennett, G.P., *The Great Road between Forth and Tay* Markinch (1983), 35
7. *O.S.A.*, 10, 366

9

The Fife Burghs and the Case of St Andrews

The influence of the burghs on the improvement of roads within their bounds can be traced further back in time than can the care of roads in the open country between them. In the burghs were to be found the more prosperous merchants of the county, together with artisans and their guilds, ready to give effect to communal decisions, and capable of bringing powerful sanctions to bear. Thus the streets of mediaeval Culross were paved with a raised central walkway, 'the Croun o' the Causey', where the more distinguished inhabitants could expect priority of passage.[1] At Dunfermline the baillies in 1609 'appoyntit and agreed with ane calsay bigger to com shortlie fra Edbr to this toun for repairing of ye calsayis in ye Newraw, be east ye port in ye baksyde, in ye coilzeraw and rattoun raw'. Certain baillies were deputed to 'attend upon the said wark wt power to yame to comand all ye nytbors to discharge yare nytbourlie help hereto'. Each townsman was to furnish a horse, 'and ilke nytbor wanting hors to furnish sylver'.[2]

The streets of the burghs on the coalfields were particularly subject to heavy traffic and the burgesses were also anxious to ensure ready access to the coalpits round about. A dispute between Dunfermline burgh council and the laird of Garvock over 'causeway meall' (a toll payment) is recorded in 1730, and in 1752 coal carts travelling south from the Baldridge pits were obliged to pay custom charges on entering the town. There was no serious attempt to make up the road between Dunfermline and Inverkeithing until 1756, but it is clear that a number of collieries used this route to reach the harbour, for there was an outcry when it was reported to Inverkeithing burgh council that a landowner had 'ploughed up and sowed' part of the road to Mastertown, Touch, Whitfields and the coalhills of Beath, which had been used 'past memory'.

Dysart had the mixed blessing of Lord St Clair's coal carts rumbling down the main street, but at least the owner was prepared to reinstate at his own expense a section of road past the church in 1816. Special problems were created by the ironstone carts from Lord Balfour's quarries at Balgonie, carrying their loads for shipment to the Carron foundry across the Forth. The venture had failed by 1817, but for many years complaints were received by the Kirkcaldy road trustees that the road immediately north of Dysart had been cut up as a result of the 'great traffic by ironstone carriages'.

Beyond the coalfields there could still be heavy traffic from supplies of food, coal and materials for textile manufacture. At Cupar in 1698 the burgh council, concerned to keep the streets free from obstruction, asked that the minister should 'advertise to the people' from the pulpit that 'all public vennels were to be made patent', and in 1713 supplies of sand and gravel were requisitioned for repairing the 'cassae fra the brig to the miln gate port'. Between the same port and Cupar mills the road needed repair in 1750 when the town council ordered 'that every Burgess within this Burgh as they shall be called by the Baillies, shall give, either by themselves or one Imployed for them, a full day's work gratis or pay sixpence in lieu thereof, and that everyone that has a cart within the Burgh shall give a full yoaking of four hours also gratis to such work'.

St Andrews and the roads of the East Neuk

In terms of their relation to the overall pattern of the county's road system, it is interesting to compare the four principal centres on which the four presbyteries and later the four road districts were based. Dunfermline and Cupar lie at the intersections of several routeways, exhibiting a radial pattern with strong east-west axes. In the cases of Kirkcaldy and St Andrews, the coastal locations confine the pattern to semi-circles. However, there are important differences to be noted, resulting from the ways in which the road systems developed. While the two coastal towns were, in the mid-eighteenth century, roughly comparable in population size, Kirkcaldy's primary function had been that of a port, and connections with its hinterland were based on commercial factors, particularly the movement of coal and the export of agricultural products. The least productive areas were only feebly supplied with roads, particularly towards the north-west in the direction of Loch Leven, where, but for the coal workings at Cluny and the enterprise of Rothes and Ferguson, a large area would long have remained virtually roadless. While Leslie did become linked with Kirkcaldy by a good statute labour road at a late stage, it was found easier to travel east to the Great Road at Cadham and then south, as at present.

By contrast, St Andrews developed as a route centre early in the mediaeval period, a place of pilgrimage rather than a port serving the neighbouring countryside. On a modern road map of eastern Fife the strongly developed radial pattern of the connections between St Andrews and the south coast is striking. Links to the market centre of Cupar, to the Kinghorn ferry by way of Ceres, and to the Dundee ferries by Guardbridge, complete the impression of regional dominance, with few settlements of any size to be seen between St Andrews and the periphery of the East Neuk.

Yet at a time when the other larger towns were expanding and manufacturing industries were being set up, St Andrews lagged behind, and activity in terms of road improvement was slow. At the end of the eighteenth century the ancient city was only beginning to emerge from a long period of economic stagnation and depopulation. This period of decline, which may well have extended back into the seventeenth century, can be contrasted with accounts of the city 'in the meridian of its glory', up to the beginning of the Protestant Reformation, when it was an ecclesiastical centre for Scotland, with a flourishing university and many overseas contacts, both political and commercial.

Some indication of the influence of St Andrews on the establishment of a pattern of roads may be derived from the various estimates of its population size. Pennant noted that there were sixty bakers in the sixteenth century as against twelve when he wrote in 1776. The 'Senzie Market' was held within the Priory at that time, for which 'two or three hundred vessels were generally seen to arrive', with merchants from most of the trading kingdoms of Europe. If an estimate by Bishop Spottiswoode, who was in office between 1615 and 1639, is to be believed, there could have been as many as 15,000 inhabitants in 1560. The first blow came when the people were 'terribly thinned by the pest' in 1585. A contemporary account describes the plague as breaking out in St Andrews with a loss of over 4,000 lives, 'and the place was left almost desolate'. Thomas Tucker in 1655, noting that the town had 'formerly been bigger', cast his eye as a customs officer over the disused harbour and doubtless deplored the loss of revenue.[3]

A further decline in the town's fortunes, both in terms of prosperity and numbers, may be attributed to the loss of the episcopacy in 1688, and by 1697 the town had become so unattractive that it was suggested the University should be moved to Perth, an act which would have made St Andrews 'no more than a fishing village'.[4] In 1728 some 4,000 inhabitants were said to be living in only 945 out of a total of 1,104 houses, the remainder being in ruins.

A more optimistic picture is presented by the parish minister's report in 1793, when, although the population of the town itself was given as only 2,854, he sees the town's emergence 'by the spirited exertions of a few individuals'. A contemporary writer also expressed the hope that St Andrews would 'again rise to a degree of respectability from trade and manufactures'.

Pruning the Surplus Branches

Despite the previous period of decline, the roads that displayed the town as a focus of communications were still there, although numerous radiating routes were being eliminated by the concentration of traffic on those which received some sort of maintenance and those on which fords had been replaced by bridges. Whatever might have been lacking in St Andrews itself, the East Neuk by the end of the eighteenth century was an area of small but enterprising lairds, where prospects for agricultural improvement were good, especially along the coastal belt between Largo and Crail. Even in the 1720s these proprietors were among the most active in Fife in securing their share of any county funds. Of the deliberations of these gentlemen within the statute labour district of St Andrews we know little, and it is probable that such improvements as there were took place as a result of the initiative of individuals on their own estates, and records were not kept of how the labour services or money were spent. Certainly there were changes between the time of Roy's survey (1755) and Ainslie's map (1775). The old road from Anstruther through Lambieletham and down along the burn past Pipeland has only survived in places today, and the ridge road from Cupar through Radernie and Knights Ward to Kingsbarns can only be traced with difficulty.

In 1221 the Priory at St Andrews was responsible for a dependent foundation at Pittenweem, and evidence of a direct road link to that town is provided in a simple map by Nicholls of 1710 (Fig. 9.1). The existence of such a road in 1734 is suggested by a petition to the Fife commissioners of supply asking for a road 'by Pittarthie' to be repaired. It was unsuccessful, but it may be that the route indicated by Nicholls passed the seventeenth-century tower house of that name (Figs. 9.2 and 9.3). A road on Roy's map follows part of the same line, at least as far north as the Kinaldy Burn near Tosh, but it then turns north-westwards to pass near the old site of Gilmerton House and takes a new

Figure 9.1

PART OF MAP BY NICHOLLS c.1710

Fig. 9.2. Pittarthie Castle from the old Pittenweem road. A petition in 1734 for repair of this road appears to have been ignored, effectually discontinuing its use. The way to St Andrews passed near the tower house on the skyline, left.

Fig. 9.3. Pittarthie Castle. An example of the less defensive type of residence appearing in the mid-17th century. The date over the window in the eastern extension is 1653.

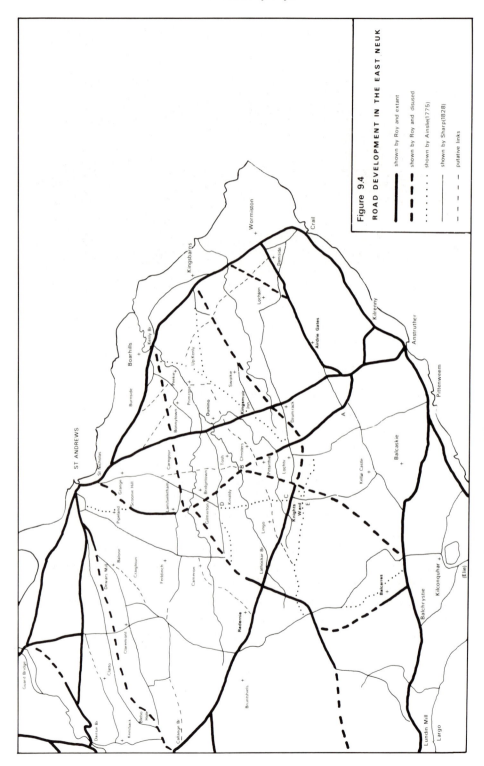

Figure 9.4
ROAD DEVELOPMENT IN THE EAST NEUK

Fig. 9.5. Peekie Bridge from the north. Travellers from St Andrews to Crail had to take a sharp right-angle turn at the cliff face before proceeding along the south bank of the Kenly Burn. Peekie Mill is to the right.

alignment similar to the modern Lambieletham road towards St Andrews. Having surmounted Scoonie Hill, it does not follow the Pipeland road, shown twenty years later by Ainslie, but swings across to St Nicholas (Fig. 9.4).

These two swings in direction might well be explained by the freedom, in 1755, to choose those parts of established routes that were in the least state of disrepair, as would be perfectly possible in a largely unenclosed landscape. Pennant's account of his departure from St Andrews in 1776 in which he finds 'the country on the heights very uncultivated and full of moors' is consistent with this supposition.

One reason for the abandonment of several of the intermediate radial roads leading south from St Andrews was the problem of crossing the west to east flowing burns. The present road to Largo runs where their upper sections are easily fordable and where the ridges in between the burns present only gentle gradients, whereas the road to Anstruther has needed bridges because the burns are entrenched in steep-sided dens. The Pittarthie road came in between the two — not worth building bridges for, but with difficult fording places after heavy rainfall. This

Fig. 9.6. Peekie Bridge: armorial panel. The arms are those of Prior Hepburn, who was in office in 1500.

would not be found satisfactory as wheeled traffic became more common, and the road would have become disused.

Further east, the St Andrews to Crail road has to cross the Kenly Burn, which carries the combined waters of the two burns crossed by the Anstruther road. The present bridge carries the date 1793 and is only one of several extant or former bridges built between Boarhills and Dunino. One handsome structure, finished with interlocking coping stones at Peekie (560126), is now quite disused. It bears the arms of Prior Hepburn, who was in office from 1488 to 1517 (Figs. 9.5 and 9.6). In 1512 a hospital originally intended for the reception of pilgrims visiting the relics of St Andrew was found to have outlived its purpose, and in these premises Prior Hepburn established the college of St Leonards. Among the lands provided for the support of the college were those of Peekie, from which millers of the parish were bringing loads into the city in 1597. While the road over Peekie Bridge can be followed by a sequence of rights of way into Crail, it is clear that the bridge had its limitations, including the abrupt right-angle turn that had to be made on the south side where there is a vertical sandstone cliff. A replacement was built further downstream, of which the

Fig. 9.7. The Bishop's Road from Drumcarrow. The dotted line follows the road along a low ridge and the cross marks the site of the murder.

present Kenly Bridge was probably a successor.

In the remaining sector of the radial pattern centred on St Andrews are the routes from the city to Ceres, by Dairsie Bridge to Cupar and the road by Guardbridge to Dundee. Only the first of these has been the subject of a major realignment, and the change has followed the pattern, familiar in upland areas, of the replacement of a ridge route by one at a lower level. The original 'Bishop's Road', named from its association with the death of Archbishop Sharp when his coach was crossing Magus Muir in 1679, may be traced on the ground from Dewars Mill (478159) to Blebo Hole (424135) (Figs. 9.7 and 9.8). It appears on the maps of Roy and Ainslie, but the building of the turnpike roads to the north and south of the ridge (Roads 47 and 48 of the 1807 Act) caused Sharp to omit the old road from his map in 1828. Efforts have been made to close sections of it as a right of way although the county statute labour trustees confirmed its continued use for farm traffic in 1826. The old ridge road is bounded on one side in a section south of Morton (432147) by a dyke with exceptionally large boulders, a possible indication that it was contemporary with an early stage in the enclosure of adjacent land.

Fig. 9.8. The Bishop's Road from Road 48. A narrow belt of woodland marks the ridge road and a monument to the Archbishop is to be found in the wood to the right, part of Magus Muir.

Road Management in the East Neuk

During St Andrew's slow recovery from its post-Reformation torpor, it would not be expected that the town would exercise much influence upon the landowners in the surrounding countryside who were managing the roads. As statute labour trustees for St Andrews district under the 1774 Act, there was no particular reason why they should do more than observe the minimum requirements of the law in applying the statute labour or keeping accounts. Usually the clerk to the burgh council doubled as clerk to the trustees, but the incumbent at St Andrews already had his hands full in seeing that the streets were repaired, the statute labour for which, in 1782, had to be authorised by the district trustees. The sum of five pounds was granted to the town, provided that the inhabitants subscribed an equal amount. Ten years later the town was induced to contribute ten guineas towards the new turnpike road to Guardbridge, but claimed this was as much as it could afford.

The trustees were a shadowy body whose joint decisions seldom

Fig. 9.9. Dairsie Bridge, late 18th century. The Arms of Archbishop Beaton, c.1521, are in the left spandrel. The boundary between St Andrews and Cupar districts ran along the River Eden at this point and the bridge was maintained jointly.

appeared in the records of the county. The district remained predominantly rural in character and the demands of traffic on the roads changed but slowly. The burghs of the south coast used their local autonomy to keep the streets and roads in their immediate neighbourhoods in tolerable repair, but elsewhere what was done depended on the initiative of individual landowners. If the more opportunistic, such as the Earl of Balcarres, could make use of public money to benefit roads adjoining their property, so much the better. Otherwise, the heritors were left to get on as best they might with the administration of the sections of road placed in their charge.

Some of their activities come to light in the latter part of the eighteenth century when they impinge on the neighbouring districts. Thus in 1787 the district was asked to help with the cost of repairs to Dairsie Bridge (Fig. 9.9) which lay on their boundary. It seems that the roads in Kemback parish, which was in St Andrews district, had been taken over by Cupar, and the product of the ploughgate (unit of area) levy for the statute labour fund had been sequestered for this purpose. The sum was not enough to repair both the Kemback roads and the bridge, hence the necessity for the request. This does suggest that where it was possible to delegate the repair of marginal roads, which the St Andrews trustees would rather not be bothered with, to their better organised neighbour, this is what happened. In the same way, a road through Leuchars parish was being built in 1787 with only a monetary contribution from St Andrews district, the actual work being carried out by Cupar. In 1792 a proportion of the revenue of Guardbridge tollbar was allocated by Cupar trustees to a St Andrews road, and they also were responsible for instructing a surveyor to report on the roads in that district. St Andrews, it seems, either lacked the ability or the inclination to manage these affairs.

There were, however, certain inescapable duties required by statute. The 1774 Act asked for a list of ploughgates to be kept, and the 1797 Act required a list of statute labour roads to be submitted to the annual county meeting of trustees. This was done by St Andrews in 1798. The involvement of the district in the expanding turnpike system was at first limited to those roads in the 1790 and 1797 Acts which happened to cross its boundaries. The first of these, Road 4, ran from Leven to Crail, with a tollbar at Lundin Mill set up by a county meeting and its income noted in Cupar minutes; this confirms a suspicion that in St Andrews district no more than rudimentary administrative procedures were observed, and the usual accounts or minute book might even have been dispensed with. Again, under the 1807 Turnpike Act, in which Roads 42 to 54 came within St Andrews district, a number of tollbars were set up, but the supervising committees were appointed by the county meeting and not by St Andrews. Eventually, in 1815, the district was prevailed upon to organise the annual roup of its own tollbars, either at St Andrews or at Colinsburgh.

It is perhaps significant that the earliest statute labour records date from the year before sections 14 and 15 of the General Turnpike Act of 1823 made their keeping compulsory. Further encouragement for the observance of correct procedures was provided by the Fife Turnpike Act of 1829 in which the clerk and treasurer each became liable to a £50 penalty in the case of inexact accounts and had to submit the accounts annually to an auditor. In spite of these strictures, some turnpike business continued to appear in the statue labour books and certain trustees were chronically disinclined to present their accounts.

Administrative Reforms

Nevertheless, there is evidence in the 1820s of a tightening-up of administration. Alleged mismanagement of roads in Cameron parish was investigated by the Statute Labour Trustees, and an over-generous allowance to Lindsey of Feddinch was cut down. Surveyors were employed for three divisions of the district in 1822, and responsibility was accepted for repaving South Street, St Andrews. The influence of Captain Playfair may be seen in this, for he contributed £50 towards the fund of £350 and was put on the appropriate committee.

Full accounts were printed and distributed to trustees in 1831 and a map of all the roads of the district was completed by the land surveyor John Duncan in 1834. In spite of these manifestations of efficiency General Durham of Largo saw further room for improvement. 'The present system of management', he said, 'is highly objectionable and imperfect and not calculated to effect the object which it aimed at.' After which he revealed that he had lately met Mr McConnell of the McAdam partnership and been deeply impressed.

McConnell was promptly engaged and in two years had reorganised the road management. He was fortunate in that the turnpike roads were paying well, the revenue from St Andrews district tolls having been £3,311 in 1828, second only to Cupar with £3,464. In 1835 McConnell produced detailed reports on all roads in the district, each of which was listed with its length and the expenditure required in the coming year. Having observed the benefits of this style of management, Kirkcaldy district was to follow the lead of St Andrews in 1837, but Cupar and Dunfermline continued under the direction of their existing surveyors.

When he was asked in 1844 to give his recommendations on proposed reductions in the statute labour assessment and of tolls, together with the advisability of changing the number and distribution of tolls, McConnell's findings were taken up by Pagan as an example of the difficulties encountered by a turnpike district. Presenting the report of the investigating committee, Lord Douglas described the geographical situation of St Andrews, whose 'insular position' (sic) deprived it of the great traffic which as thoroughfares the other districts possessed — it had few seats of manufacture and no great extent of commerce; having the sea on three sides the carriage for commercial purposes was chiefly on water and consequently the sources to which the district had mainly to look for the support of its roads were agricultural traffic, ploughgate assessments, tollgates to catch agricultural and other produce on their way to seaports, the import of mercantile commodities and coal, and traffic from the west.

Douglas pointed out that the tollgates had been established 'when the roads were not all in the same state of keeping — when their condition depended on the different degrees of skill and attention which different individuals happened to possess and bestow, and where debts are mostly increasing. Now when things were otherwise', he continued, 'the produce of the tolls (were) applied alike to all parts of the district. Why should not the toll-bars [now] be put in better positions?' It seemed to him, for instance, that there was no fairness in taxing Anstruther, Pittenweem and Elie as sea ports and allowing Crail, Largo and St Andrews, on its southern side, to escape toll-free. There should be extra tollbars at Crail, at Largo, and at Feddinch, south of St Andrews.

After a lengthy discussion the St Andrews trustees voted to reject the Douglas committee's proposals. A fresh attempt was made to introduce the extra tollbars in 1841, which was narrowly successful, but in an adjourned meeting the decision was reversed. Pagan comments, 'Such was the fruitless result, and will often be the fate, of attempts to give fair play to the toll-bar system. When once a road is made, and people are accustomed to use it toll-free, they abhor the idea of a tax being imposed upon it, and immediately rise in open arms against such a proposal, however equitable it may be'. He acknowledges, however, that additional bars were later placed at Kingsbarns and Lochton.

With the relatively unchanged pattern of traffic movement the roads which were to be found at the end of the 1840s differed little from those shown on Ainslie's map. In fact the replacement of the Bishop's Road to Pitscottie by Roads 48 and 80 was the principal alteration. With a reliable flow of traffic and few major realignments, the district was in a better position to cope with the coming of the railway. By the time negotiations with the railway companies had to be considered, a sub-committee in 1846 was able to report that, whereas other turnpike trusts had unprofitable roads and little prospect of paying off their debts unless they assigned their tolls to the railway, the St Andrews trust was in a position to demand compensation for any loss of tolls that might result from its operations. The latter did not in fact take place until 1854, when the newly formed East of Fife Railway commenced its negotiations.[5]

NOTES

1. Cunningham, A.S., *Culross, Past and Present* Leven (1910), 63

2. Shearer, A. (ed.), *Burgh Records of Dunfermline in the sixteenth and seventeenth centuries* Dunfermline (1951), 130

3. Robertson, E.S., *Old St Andrews* London (1923), 271

4. Lyon, C.J., *History of St Andrews* London (1843), 119

5. Bruce, W.S., *The Railways of Fife* Perth (1980), 97

10

The Evolution of the Modern Road System

The collapse of coach services wherever the railway system began to extend in the late 1840s was an event which should not be allowed to loom too large when viewing the county's subsequent road development. We have seen how the most important roads had already been established by the beginning of the eighteenth century. What then occurred was a period of bridge-building, associated with a concentration of traffic along the best-situated roads. Hill routes tended to be abandoned in favour of valleys as soon as resources became available for drainage and the building of new roads. Much of the reconstruction of the earlier pattern took place in the half-century between 1790 and 1840, a surprising amount of preliminary work having been carried out before any money from tolls began to come in.

It was only at the end of this fifty-year period that fast passenger coaches appeared on the scene, the removal of exemption from mail coaches in 1813 providing funds to repair the damage they caused. In the 1830s, when coach services had reached their fullest development, railways were already being established in England; many of the Fife turnpike trustees, while recognising the problems with which the trusts would be faced, clearly recognised that, on balance, the faster and cheaper transport offered by the railways would bring them greater benefits in other ways. Referring to a request made in 1830 for government assistance to improve the Great North Road, Sir George Campbell of Edenswood said this would be largely a waste of money, for it was obvious that the best means of communication in the future would be the railway. In 1840, when details of the new low-water pier at Burntisland were being discussed, it was pointed out that only with the provision of a railway could the full benefits be realised.

Pagan was undismayed by the effects of reduced road traffic on the profitability of the tollbars he despised. After all, he argued, 'coaching on toll roads pays only betwixt very populous towns, as the high fares consequent on the tolls preclude the mass of the community from ever presuming to set foot in a coach'. The railways might have reduced coach tolls 'nearly to zero', but they were 'giving an immense impetus to travelling and to commerce'. He foresaw a greater number of horses being employed on numerous short journeys, which would increase the revenue from his proposed horse tax. There would be an increase of 'cross public conveyances between one town and another', and each locality would 'have its stage-coach, or omnibus, or fly, unless provided with railway conveyance', when tolls were abolished.

A malodorous area of competition was revealed when a carter wrote to the surveyor of Kirkcaldy district: 'Dear Sir, I am thinking of driving swine dung to Fosterton by carts. Will you allow me to pass Kirkcaldy Turnpike and Gallowtown for 2d per cart — the Rail takes it for 1s 3d per ton, but a man has engaged to cart down some hundreds of cart loads of bricks from Redford and is willing to cart up my dung, if I can get the Toll for 2d per cart. Please reply – it is all gain to you, as otherwise it goes by Rail and you do not get anything. Yours, etc. Robert Hutchinson'. The Committee declined 'acceding to Mr Hutchinson's proposal'.

In a desperate effort to make ends meet, Pagan suspects that the trustees would be tempted to set up more and more tollbars to catch less and less traffic; the tollkeepers would be getting daily more numerous but not less hungry. If their wages were not increased, he warned, they might even go on strike. However, if the country could only be persuaded to give up tollbars he envisaged a golden era of freedom where districts beyond the railway network would have their transport services rejuvenated, for they would become valuable feeders to their nearest stations.

A committee was appointed by the Fife county road trustees in 1846 to report on their examination of Mr Pagan's proposals. While not commenting on the merits of his tax on horse-power, they accepted most of his criticisms of the existing system — the unequal burden on road users, how tolls were unrelated to the damage that was caused, and the ease of evasion. The committee were of the opinion 'that these evils might be remedied by the substitution of a measure of local taxation; to which remedy, if the imperfections of the present system do not urge the trustees, it is possible that the change in the through traffic caused by the railways now in progress and contemplated, will at no late period render it expedient to resort'. The committee reported again in 1847, with the results of a study of two contrasting parishes, Scoonie, a burgh with considerable manufacture and a population of 2,640, and Logie, an agricultural parish with only 410 people. To provide the same revenue as was being obtained from tolls and statute labour payments, the 161 Scoonie horses would have to pay a tax of £3.7.0 each, and the 75 in Logie £1.12.2. If on the other hand they were to introduce a rate on current real rents, the rate in Scoonie would have to be 1s 2½d in the pound, and in Logie 8d. Despite such anomalies the committee was inclined towards some form of local taxation, but the meeting was not prepared to take any action. They would wait and see what the effect of the railways would be; meanwhile the report would be allowed to 'lie on the table'. Pagan, with masterful restraint, records merely that 'Fife contemplates the possibility of a change of some kind or other, some day or other . . .'

Meanwhile, much of the time of the road trustees in the late 1840s was being taken up by questions of compensation for loss of toll revenue under terms negotiated with the railway companies and designed to remove the trusts' opposition to the railway bills going through Parliament. Alterations to roads had to be agreed, involving diversions, new bridges and level crossings. Short stretches of access road to stations were built by the railway companies themselves. Among the attempts by the road trusts to make the best of a bad situation were the movement of tollbars to catch rail-generated traffic, and charges to the railway companies for the damage done in their construction work. The Cupar trust was losing heavily on the Cupar to New Inn road since the hundreds of waggons carrying stone for the embankment west of Kingskettle managed to avoid passing either of the tolls. Pagan's answer to this was simple: 'Under our system new toll-gates and new prosecutions would be quite unnecessary. Whether fifty or five hundred horses were brought into a county for any particular work, the surveyor would immediately have them on his list, and make them pay the road rate'.

Tollkeepers were always quick to plead that a reduction of revenue entitled them to a reduction in their agreed rent of the tolls, but a vigilant surveyor could anticipate such arguments. The surveyor for Cupar reported in 1849 that 'although the traffic of some of the roads adjoining the railway has fallen off very considerably, yet the Revenue expected from the tollbars on these lines, when taken into the hands of the Trustees, has hitherto been fully realised; moreover, in consequence of there being less traffic the expenses of maintenance had been much reduced'.

The whole question of financing roads in Scotland was reviewed in 1859, when a Royal Commission was set up to examine alternative systems of assessment, both for tolls and for statute labour, which would be more economical and equitable, and also to find out whether improvements in administration could be made, for example by the consolidation of separate trusts. In a summary of the history of turnpike trusts they recalled that 'from the rapid improvement and general progress of the country, which commenced from the middle of the last century, [the statute labour system] was found to be inapplicable to the altered circumstances of the kingdom'. There had been a few instances in which roads had received government aid (such as those constructed under the Highland Commissioners for Roads and Bridges), but in general 'landed proprietors, who were materially interested in promoting a system of communication . . . in some cases made loans in expectation of safe if not a profitable investment', others were assumed to be motivated by a desire to serve the public, or wished to enhance the value of their estates.

An important distinction had to be made between the financial liabilities of the English and the Scottish turnpike trusts, in that tolls in England were applied primarily to payment of interest on the investment, whereas in Scotland such payments took second place to the repair of the roads. Creditors in England could always point to the ultimate responsibility of the parish under common law, whereas no such convenience was available in Scotland.

As an alternative to tolls the commissioners found Pagan's proposed horse tax 'neither fair nor expedient', since in their eyes 'it failed to adjust itself to the use of the roads by individuals so rated'. Pagan, giving evidence, said he now agreed that a new valuation act was needed and that 'ingenuity can never arrive at any system of tolls which would make parties pay for the roads according to the use they make of them'.

Counties were urged in the report to set up county road boards employing their own surveyors, and it was noted that several counties might share the same head surveyor, as was already the case with the growing practice of the McAdam-McConnell partnership. From the submissions of witnesses from all over Scotland, it was evident that the majority were in favour of the abolition of tolls and a Bill was presented the same year to this effect. Legislation was, however, delayed until 1878, when a General Act provided for the county road boards to be created. Each county was free to decide on the timescale for the abolition of tolls and of statute labour, with a deadline in 1883.[1]

The response of Fife was immediate and the last meeting of the county turnpike trustees took place on 7th May 1878. For the time being the commissioners of supply acted as county road trustees, to be replaced in 1889 by the newly formed county councils, the ultimate power of decision on matters of road management now being in the hands of elected representatives of the road users. The subsequent division of responsibility and sources of funding between the county, or its recent successor the region, and central government is outwith the scope of this book, but a brief summary of the physical developments in the road system would be appropriate.

The New Traffic

Although improvements in the remainder of the nineteenth century were mainly confined to adaptations to railway traffic — access roads, bridges and level crossings — the pattern of movement and the volume of traffic were locally much affected by the railway system as it expanded. The Broad Ferry from Granton to Burntisland became the first choice for traffic from south of the Forth, particularly when the 'floating railway' — a ferry boat built to carry a whole train — was introduced in 1850. The number of passengers using the Queensferry crossing dwindled. Even if their destination had been Perth, they could now join the Great North Road by the improved connection between Burntisland and Cowdenbeath (Road 63).

When the railway bridges came to be built across the Tay (1878,[2] 1888) and the Forth (1889), the flow of vehicles and passengers to the ferry piers became a trickle, consisting almost entirely of local traffic. The roads of Fife, relieved of much of the previous wear and tear, slumbered on, with the trustees, and their successors the district council surveyors, attending to routine maintenance up to the time when the number of motor vehicles began to increase after the First World War. Vehicles with rubber tyres greatly reduced the damage done to the surface as compared with the iron rims of wheels and horses' hooves, while the stabilising and waterproofing effect of bitumenised surfacing, developed in the 1880s — 'tarmacadam' — steadily increased the comfort of travel and reduced maintenance costs. It is perhaps ironical that the process should have been named after a man whose failure as a tar manufacturer, from lack of demand for his product, should have prompted him to dedicate the rest of his life to the problems of road maintenance.[3]

The dangers from large numbers of fast-moving vehicles were not new to the road authorities; demands for road widening and the easing of sharp bends were heard at the meetings of trustees long before the age of the internal combustion engine.

The forestairs along the main street in Kirkcaldy were pulled down when the street, only thirteen feet wide in some places, had to be widened in 1823. It was said to be particularly dangerous when smoke from the salt pans 'falls down upon the street and prevents passengers seeing their way above a yard or two'. In 1864 concern for public safety at a narrow bend in Falkland prompted a petition to the burgh council. The risk of collision when two vehicles tried to pass one another at this point caused parents to fear for the safety of their children 'who pass and repass twice daily to the Parish School'. Other inhabitants held to be in danger were the crowds going home from the churches on Sundays, and pedestrians at night who experienced 'very painful feelings when horses or vehicles were heard approaching'. By agreement with the owner the offending houses were pulled down and the road was widened, but we are not told how painful were the feelings of the former occupants.[4]

It was to be another fifty years before the speed of vehicles began to call for gentle curves and unobstructed vision, for horseless carriages remained a novelty in many parts of Scotland. Indeed, the last stage-coach was still in service in 1914 between Kingussie and Loch Laggan. The motor bus which succeeded it had to run at times which avoided encounters with the mail coach, until the latter was withdrawn the following year.[5]

Widening of streets and the provision of bypasses for the new traffic continued to modify in detail the pattern of Fife roads through the inter-war period. But it was not until the years of reconstruction after 1945 that any major new roads were planned, with the aim of reducing journey times and to stimulate the local economy. In a report of 1946 a planning advisory committee of Fife County Council stated: 'The system of roads as it exists today in Fife was developed during the eighteenth and nineteenth centuries. The main routes then laid down still exist, but with the advent and great increase of motor traffic they are no longer entirely adequate as regards surface and width of carriageway'.[6] The removal of obstacles to traffic flow, the provision of dual carriageways and the segregation of pedestrians were recommended; and there was a warning against bypasses close enough to centres of population to encourage ribbon development. Even where the latter could be controlled by the limited legislation of the time, the effect was only temporary and 'the mounting ground cost would finally swallow up the bypass into the developed area'.

The first surge of new traffic in Fife brought by road improvements came from the west when, in 1937, the opening of the swing bridge at Kincardine cut out the long detour to Stirling, which heavy loads had to make to reach Dunfermline from Edinburgh. There still were, of course, the ferries at Kinghorn and at Queensferry, but these were judged to take only an insignificant part of the total traffic. For loads between Edinburgh and Dundee the bridges at Kincardine and Perth meant a journey of about eighty-five miles, as against fifty-three miles if the passages at Queensferry and Newport could be used. By the 1960s the convenience of travel by private car had come to outweigh the advantages of the railway, and both these ferries were again becoming congested at times; before replacement by the Forth Road Bridge the Queen's Ferry was carrying over two million passengers and 900,000 cars a year.[7]

The question of road bridges across the Forth and the Tay had been foremost in the minds of those who, in 1946, saw improved road communications as the key to the future prosperity of the region. There was little argument as to the crossing place on the Forth, and there was no revival of the plan for a tunnel put forward at the time the rail bridge was being planned. While an artist's impression of the road bridge was included as a frontispiece in the 1946 report, the eventual structure completed in 1964 was of a much lighter appearance. By this time the system of motorways pioneered with the M1 in England in the late 1950s had extended into Scotland.

Of the through roads proposed in the 1946 Fife report (Fig. 11.1), only one has yet been completed — that from the Forth Road Bridge to Kinross and Perth, the M90. The story of the various schemes to connect the Great North Road to the Great Road through Fife is still not complete, and will be recounted in the next chapter. Roads planned in 1946 to bypass Dunfermline, Leven and Leuchars have been built, and a whole new network of roads has also been laid out for the new town at Glenrothes. However, the bypasses planned for Kennoway, Auchtermuchty, Cupar and St Andrews (Fig. 11.1) have not materialised.

Two sites for a road bridge across the Tay were being considered in 1946, and the Council reported that 'the opinion in the industrial areas of Fife and generally the region to the north-west is decidedly in favour of a bridge at Newburgh rather than at Newport'. Although one would have had to travel another five miles to reach Dundee over a bridge in the western position, it was argued that there would be a substantial saving in the cost of construction, and it would stimulate development

F

in the otherwise neglected area of Fife between New Inn and Newburgh. This was the option recorded as most popular with those attending the public meetings held at Inverkeithing, Lochgelly and St Andrews. It is notable that the burghs of Newport and Tayport preferred a position for a bridge further up river than the railway bridge. An ex-provost was quoted as saying that Newport was quite satisfied to be a residential burgh and to be called the 'Dormitory of Dundee', but he acknowledged that Newport could expect to have very little say as to where the new bridge was to be situated. Nobody at these meetings seems to have anticipated that when the bridge was completed the irksome system of tolls was to be reintroduced to Fife, and the battle for their abolition would have to begin all over again.

NOTES

1. Ferguson, J., *The Law of Roads, Streets and Rights of Way in Scotland* Edinburgh (1904), 117

2. Sir Thomas Bouch's bridge collapsed during a gale in December 1879. See: Bruce, W.S., *The Railways of Fife* Perth (1980), 169

3. Reader, W.J., *MacAdam: The McAdam Family and the Turnpike Roads 1798-1861* London (1980), 27

4. Bennett, G.P., *The Great Road between Forth and Tay* Markinch (1983), 33

5. Gardiner, L., *Stage-Coach to John O'Groats* London (1961), 204

6. Fife County Council, *Fife Looks Ahead* Edinburgh (1946), 110

7. Dean, P. and C., *Passage of Time* North Queensferry (1981), 75

11

The Legacy of the Early Roads and Their Planners

As has been seen, the main thrust of road development in Fife has been across the peninsula, from south to north, with relatively little effort devoted to connections from west to east. This is hardly surprising, since the former roads expressed the desires of travellers on a national scale, whereas the peninsula was, by definition, a dead-end.

At St Andrews, once the authority of the old Church had been largely destroyed and the motivation of pilgrims removed, there was little to take its place as a magnet for travellers, except for a small university struggling for survival and the nascent pastime of golf. Only at the end of the eighteenth century did St Andrews become a town to be visited as a coastal resort, the council discussing the erection of 'a sea bathing house for visitors' as early as 1784.

East-West Links

South of the axial ridge stretching from the West Lomond, the fishing ports of the East Neuk had traditionally looked first to the sea for transport. Cupar was well enough served by roads to fulfil its functions as a market town and centre of administration; the importance of a highway to Kinross through Auchtermuchty had been noted in 1723, but when it came to finding subscribers for a road of turnpike standard after 1790 (Road 10), it will be remembered that the county had to appeal to the heritors of Kinross and form a joint trust before the money was forthcoming (p. 103).

Interest in better communications between the western district of Fife, centred on Dunfermline, and the rest of the county has at times been ambivalent. The principal concerns of the baillies of Dunfermline and Inverkeithing up to the middle of the eighteenth century were the sale of coal and the supply of the linen industry. The transport for both was primarily directed towards the Forth. The baillies of Dunfermline are found in 1641 to be considering 'how necesar it is that coalles be caried from Pittincreiff to the Limekills to the effect that the samen may be barkit at that port in the same selff ship or bark yt sall happine to leve the sklaites[1] at Lymkills'. In 1753, the year that the first turnpike bill affecting Fife was being discussed, the Provost of Inverkeithing wrote to more than seventeen members of parliament to ensure that panwood, or coal carried to heat the salt pans, should be exempted from tolls, and that other coal would be charged according to the distance travelled. In one letter he writes, 'We see by yours to the Magistrates of Dunfermline that the Gentlemen in the east of Fife wants a Turnpike road bet this toun and Kinghorn, which, if obtained, we are convinced will be a great hardship to this toun'. The recipient was asked to do all he could to prevent it.

Yet in 1756 it was reported to the Dunfermline Burgh Council that the Justices had met 'with a great many of the principal inhabitants By south the Town's parks in order to Consent the proper way of Carying the high Road from the East End of the Toun towards Kirkaldie by the South of the said park dykes'. The route chosen was that proposed for turnpike road No.5 of the 1790 Act, and lay along ridges through Crossgates and Auchtertool to Kirkcaldy — hilly, but relatively firm and dry. Under the management of Ferguson of Raith a tollbar was erected at Baidlin in 1795.

Across the poorly endowed area north-west of Kirkcaldy road provision was niggardly; of the parish reports in the 1790s, that for Auchterderran expresses the sense of neglect: 'The roads hitherto made were done by statute-labour, but are very indifferent'. Welcoming the prospect of the turnpike road described in the Act as 'the Road from the Plaisterer's by Kinglassie, Auchterderran and the Kirk of Beath' (Road 8 of Fig. 5.4), the minister notes that 'this line of road is already in use in the summer months, but a free communication through this inland district would be highly advantageous. The general opinion of the common people is not against turnpikes. This parish has hitherto been distinguished for bad roads, and is inaccessible on the north for six months in the year. Hence the farmers on the opposite side must sell their commodities at an under rate, being shut out from the coast towns'.

Of the roads listed in the successive turnpike acts, a number could not be identified as having subsequently become toll roads and in some cases were never built at all. Few roads aroused so much local interest or experienced such a protracted series of delays in their execution as the Kirk of Beath to Plasterer's Inn road. The inn, just south of Balbirnie Bridge, would have been well known from many a thirsty journey to those Fife landowners whose assent was required before a road could be included in the forthcoming turnpike bill. The Kirk of

Beath, on its isolated hilltop site, 'a most fitt and convenient place . . . being upone the roade way, and in the just midis betwixt Kinross and Innerkethine', could be named with equal confidence as the other terminus. The road was greatly desired by the landowners in the parishes abutting the Kinross border: Beath, Ballingry, Auchterderran and Kinglassie. Among the most active among these gentlemen as road trustees were those for whom a new road would reduce the cost of distributing coal from pits on their lands, particularly Syme of Lochore, Ferguson of Cluny and Raith, and Sir Gilbert Elliot of Lochgelly. Elliot took an active part in the drafting of the 1790 Act and appears to have been the principal coordinator of the local demand for a better east-west route.

So sure were the drafters of the parliamentary bill that the new road would be built that they prescribed a junction with a proposed road north from Kirkcaldy through Cluny (Road 9). The latter was soon completed, and a tollbar was erected south of Cluny coal pits to catch the lucrative traffic taking coal to Kirkcaldy harbour for export. Unfortunately, the road from the Plasterers to the Kirk of Beath had not the same commercial prospects, and was going to require a greater effort to win support. It is not until 1804 that we find evidence of a serious commitment to starting work on the road. At that time Gilbert Elliot, Lord Minto, who had married the daughter of Lochgelly House, was clearly trying to drum up financial support for a road passing through their estate. He was temporarily exasperated with a neighbour, Syme of Lochore, a writer to the Signet, whom he suspected of obstructing the plan, quarrelling with the committee and liable to withdraw his subscription. 'In which case', Minto writes, 'we must either pay the piper or have no road'. Otherwise, he claims, 'everything is settled — the trustees having consented to placing two [toll] gates upon it'.

The letter was in draft form, and was probably never sent, which would have been just as well. 'It might be begun tomorrow', he continues, 'if Mr Syme was not either crazy or worse. He says he will not subscribe if there is any committee and I am told he cannot lay down the first half of his subscription, being certainly distressed and his affairs in great confusion. I find he for some years has been deranged himself as well as his affairs, owing to a fall from his horse four or five years ago, and on that account was obliged to quit his profession. He has never attended any meeting tho' always promising and always summoned, and he has done all in his power to prevent this road. Measures are to be taken by the Gentlemen of the Committee . . . to bring him round if possible, of which I despair'. The intended recipient of this letter is told that even if there were no net profit from the tolls, he would get more than a five per cent return on a subscription of £1,500 from the benefits to his coal business alone. The figure for the subscription was optimistic, for it later transpired that Minto put in only £1,000 and there were no other subscriptions above £500.

In 1805 a number of letters show the maligned Mr Syme as an active and responsible road trustee who keeps in close touch with Lord Minto at his home near Jedburgh. The following year a rough estimate of £3,500 is given for the cost of the road, and the surveyor, Robert Mitchell of Largo, is asked to work out details of the proposed line. It was to start at Kirkford, just south of the Kirk of Beath, and pass north to Lochgelly through Easter Colquhally. Opinions of the turnpike trustees were divided as to whether it should then continue round the north of Auchterderran and through Kinglassie, or whether it should pass further south through Balgreggie to link up with the coal road that Ferguson of Raith was building to Thornton from Cluny.

Since it depended on the subscriptions of the principal trustees whether a scheme could succeed or fail, their views and cooperation were crucial. Absentee landowners, the prevalence of whom was deplored by parish ministers of the time, tended to be less than enthusiastic, and unreliable. One non-resident, Lord Dundas, owned land at Lumphinnans through which the new road was planned to pass, and although Syme extracted a promise to subscribe £500, Dundas was dissuaded for a time by his local factor, who regarded the sum as disproportionately generous. The farm crossed by the road was only under grass at a low rent, and the factor was suggesting that owners should contribute amounts proportional to their rent rolls, on which basis Syme and Lord Minto should be paying five or six times Dundas' subscription. Under the circumstances, he asserted, Lord Dundas could not be held to such an undertaking.

Subscribers could expect a return of up to five per cent on their investment if the tolls yielded well, but landowners were also induced to support a road by appeals to their public spirit, evidence of which brought its own rewards in terms of local prestige. These appeals, however, met with varying success; of one heritor whom Syme described as 'very rich', he commented, 'if he were not a narrow-minded miserable creature, he should give a considerable sum'. Clearly

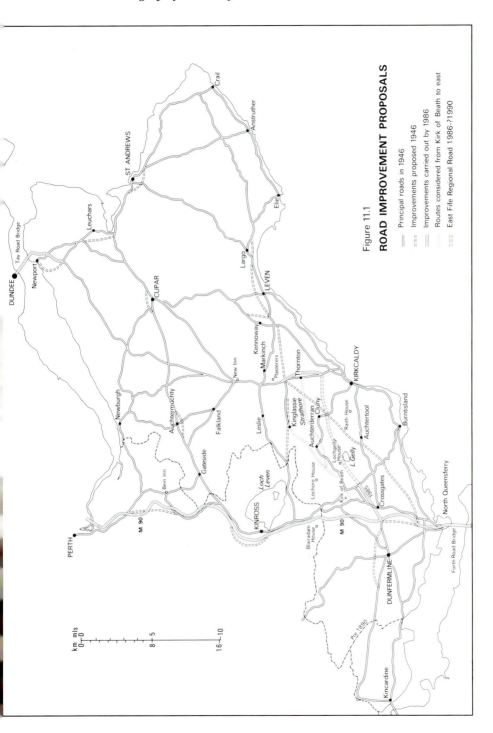

Figure 11.1

ROAD IMPROVEMENT PROPOSALS

Principal roads in 1946
Improvements proposed 1946
Improvements carried out by 1986
Routes considered from Kirk of Beath to east
East Fife Regional Road 1986-?1990

new roads provided a stage where reputations could be won or lost.

Several other lines had been suggested to the east of Auchterderran: one leading to Balfarg, another to a point half a mile south of the Plasterers, and a third finishing at Bankhead (Fig. 11.1), where the present Thornton bypass crosses the old road to Cupar. These were decisions for the trustees of Kirkcaldy district, but at the western end other interests were involved. James Loch, a nephew of William Adam of Blairadam and an experienced land factor, was one of a group of self-confessed road enthusiasts. 'Luckily for the county', he wrote, 'three or four of us have taken to new roads as our hobby, and it would surprise the more prudent and sober-minded people of the south to see with what eagerness and constancy we gallop the poor animal not over hill and dale, but round hills and through dells'. This last was of couse an allusion to the current swing away from direct routes, regardless of gradient, which was at the heart of road improvement at the time.

In a letter to Gilbert Elliot, son of Lord Minto, Loch notes that the burgh of Dunfermline, 'hearing of the revival of the plan of making the Kirk of Beath road, and being anxious to have a communication with the east of Fife that way, may probably come forward in order to have the whole go on together'. This was a reversal of the view expressed by that town in 1753, and what was proposed was a link between Dunfermline and the Great North Road through Kingseat and Micklebeath, later planned as Road 61 of the 1810 Act, which 'would come smack into the Kirk of Beath road'. Loch had warned Elliot that 'the Beath lairds' were keen to improve another road to the south 'for no reason but because no one whatever would go that way if they could'. In other words, it would be a waste of money, and he advised Elliot not to build the new road beyond the recently formed diversion of the Great North Road (Road 58 and the present A909).

In their deliberations the gentlemen of Fife had only the 1775 map by Ainslie to guide them. That, of course, had no contour lines or spot heights, and decisions had to be taken on the personal knowledge of the lie of the ground and the advice of their consultant surveyor, Robert Mitchell. Writing to Wemyss of Cuttlehill, Mitchell said he could not find the time to send him a sketch, but he advised a look at Ainslie's map and added, 'the minister of Auchter will show you where the bridge over the Ore was proposed and point out the line'. The minister, the Reverend Andrew Murray, was evidently fully conversant with these developments. As contributor to both the first and second statistical accounts, he was well qualified to keep others informed.

Loch was so concerned at having to rely on an out-of-date map that he wrote to Elliot in 1808 asking him to subscribe towards a new map of Fife 'from actual survey'. Whether Elliot did or not we are not told, but it was to be another twenty years before an accurate map, using a trigonometrical survey, was produced by Sharp, Greenwood and Fowler.

Meanwhile, Loch viewed the activities of the Fife trustees with mounting apprehension, telling Lady Minto — her husband was away in India — 'There appears to be no concert, nor any meeting of all the persons concerned, to settle the business, nor any plan, nor estimate, nor nothing'. One road trustee, James Blyth of Kinninmonth, tired of the delays and the absence of firm commitment among the other gentlemen, decided to set an example and to build a stretch of road out of his own resources – as Berry of Tayfield had done in 1803 (p. 123). This was a section just west of Kinglassie, which he regarded as no longer in dispute. He went ahead, engaging a surveyor and a contractor to build a mile of road (the present B921). It was a splendid gesture but, in the event, unwise, since before it was half finished, Ferguson of Raith had begun his coal road through Strathore (listed as Road 55 of the 1807 Act and used, briefly, by a colliery of more recent date). This had caused the trustees to change their preferred line to that through Balgreggie.

Other heritors, such as Moncrieff, owner of Harestanes, then withdrew their support from the northern line through Kinglassie, and Blyth soon realised that there was no prospect of its being finished as part of the east-west road. Writing in 1808, he remarked, 'I always thought, and still does Mr Syme, that he should have carried on the road while he had such liberal funds proffered; at least, I would have done. It is always best to strike when the iron is hottest'.

The iron had now quite definitely cooled; Lord Dundas, whose principal interest had always been in marketing the coal from his Lumphinnans pits, finally withdrew his subscription. As an absentee landlord, he did not see why he should pay for a road created primarily for the benefit of the public. The amount was not great, but it was a blow to the morale of his fellow heritors. They knew that the prospects for a return on their investment from the revenue of the tollbars were never rated highly, and there were even suggestions that the repairs to the road might not be covered by the receipts.

In spite of the setbacks, the road was mentioned for the second time in the turnpike act of 1810, this time as the terminus of Road 59, but the difficulties of securing unanimous consent to its route and of raising the necessary money appear to have been insuperable. The burgh of Dunfermline, which had initially been prepared to invest funds in a link to the Kirk of Beath, delayed any expenditure until such time as it could see the road being started to the east of the kirk. Further progress, in creating the link they now so earnestly desired with eastern Fife, had to await the establishment of a corporate local authority, armed with the power to apply tax revenue in the interests of the travelling public as a whole.

In 1836 the minister of Auchterderran was still pressing for the road to be started. The coming of the railway had already been discussed in Cupar the same year, but he does not seem to have realised what an inhibiting effect it would have on road development. The Crossgates to Thornton railway link was to be opened in 1848, and by that time any revival of the plan for an east-west road was unlikely. All that can be said is that the advent of the internal combustion engine and the pneumatic tyre lessened the inconvenience of which he complained.

The link between Auchterderran and the coal road through Strathore was never completed. The new Glenrothes ring-road through Finglassie takes a similar course to one of the alternative routes under the original plan, but west of Auchterderran there has been little attempt to replace what the minister in 1836 had termed a 'circuitous and ridgy conveyance'.[2] He confirmed that the Plasterers to Kirk of Beath road had 'never been executed', and adds, 'Several roads have since been made here with various views, but none directly or properly laying open this great thoroughfare . . . it is surprising how slowly even in this mercantile country improved lines of communication are adopted. But this direction of road will, from its obvious benefits, still force itself upon the public attention'.

We hope that the minister would approve of the East Fife Regional Road now under construction. This passes further to the south than the road planned in the late 1780s; had he heard the thunder of modern traffic, I suspect he would not have wanted it much closer to his village. Lord and Lady Minto would surely not have appreciated a high-speed dual carriageway in front of the windows of Lochgelly House.

As for Robert Mitchell the surveyor, he did point out that to have completed the road from the Kirk of Beath through Strathore to Thornton, instead of the northerly route to The Plasterers, would only have increased the journey time to Cupar by five minutes. In a car the modern traveller, using the completed East Fife Regional Road and the Thornton bypass, will be able to pass the former site of The Plasterers in an even shorter time.

Another road the minister wished to see was a revival of the old route from Burntisland, through Auchtertool and Auchterderran to Portmoak and passing east of Loch Leven to Edenshead (Gateside); thence to the Inn of Farg (Bein Inn) on the Great North Road to Perth. Indeed, such a suggestion was being made to the trustees in 1836 (p. 115). The only section of this proposed road to be built was in fact Road 74 of the 1829 Act, at the northern end, which bore a tollbar at Beansnook (161131) in 1830.

These early roads, fragments of which are still in use, are valuable in that they remind us how the shape of the landscape has influenced the choice of past routes, how alternative routes developed as local organisation and technical expertise improved, and how the needs of agricultural marketing, coal distribution and the attitudes of individual landowners influenced the flow of traffic. An understanding of these subtle forces adds a further dimension to the enjoyment of Fife.

The writer of the agricultural section in the county report in 1946[3] was certainly aware of the economic significance of abandoned roads in the modern landscape. To him, they indicated a degree of access to the more remote rural areas, greatly reduced now that they were disused. A steading is shown at Whallyden (360046) on the old road taken by Archbishop Sharp from Kennoway to Cupar, and it is pointed out that this building is now nearly half a mile from a metalled road. 'It is thought', says the report, 'that the time has come when the County should make a detailed survey of the older road system and determine which of the roads can and should be regenerated'.

In another report on the agriculture of Fife, in 1800,[4] it was said that 'The by roads are in a most deplorable state. Many parishes can derive little benefit from the great and cross roads, though in the best state of repair. Numbers of the inhabitants cannot reach a turnpike road, but with difficulty, and with scarcely half a load'.

The more recent report almost echoes these observations when it says, 'In spite of the efforts of the neighbouring owners and tenants to keep these roads in passable condition, large stretches have now become quite impassable, and many more are actually breaking down and will soon be unusable. Built . . . to carry farm carts with the usual one-ton load, these roads are now called upon to carry lorries with loads of eight, ten or twelve tons'.

Fig. 11.2. The Wallace Road, one of several roads over the Ochils between Edinburgh and Perth. In the valley is Bridge of Earn, with Moncrieff Hill beyond.

A host of physical reminders is still to be seen if the inquirer knows where to look, such as fords alongside the bridges which replaced them, bridges abandoned because unsuitably placed or inadequate for growing traffic, pieces of road unused since a railway, or even a motorway, made them redundant, milestones showing the design preferences of the different trusts and the several types of tollhouses, spaced out by the six-mile rule. There are the old quays at Pettycur, Woodhaven and North Queensferry, the last seen as we look down from the Forth Railway Bridge.

Not all these features can be preserved, but perhaps more should have public recognition and protection than is currently the case. Within the few years that I have been poking round the landscape, a bridge on the old turnpike road to Newburgh (283056) has been removed and a section of the old road to Perth from Burntisland has been obliterated by a band of pipeline trenches (191896) serving the Mossmorran petrochemical complex.

Some of the routes referred to above can be seen from modern public roads, but abandoned roads also provide some of the best walking in Scotland, and the opportunity to share what was an undoubted pleasure to early travellers — some splendid views (Figs. 11.2 to 11.4).[5]

Commenting on the tendency of early roads to be planned with very

Fig. 11.3. The Wallace Road: view towards North Fife Hills. The edges of the south-dipping lava flows cast shadows to the north.

little regard to the natural bearing of the country', one writer in 1829 added: 'Travellers had no aversion to hill-tops; they rather preferred them, because the ground was firmer to tread on and they could better see about them. On the other hand, hollows or swamps were their dread'.

For the modern traveller the question of public access arises, which, as any English visitor to Scotland comes to realise, is more a matter of courtesy than law. Following the 'country code', there are very few places the walker or horse rider would be made to feel unwelcome, but it might be better if the element of uncertainty were further reduced by the re-establishment of the old long-distance routes which a study of road history reveals.

Disused roads, even if still used as farm tracks, also form corridors for the movement of wildlife, and the old hedgerows and dykes provide reservoirs of plants and animals in a landscape increasingly threatened by the clinical efficiency of modern agriculture. There are encouraging signs that at least in some districts of Fife these matters are being taken seriously.

Fig. 11.4. The Wallace Road; detail after rain. Failure to build the carriageway up above the adjacent ground, or to maintain side ditches and cross culverts, has turned the road into a stream bed. A parallel road, the Path of Dron, was said in 1748 to be suitable only for travellers on horseback and 'no ways for Wheel Machines'. Both roads were to be superseded by a road through Glenfarg.

NOTES

1. Shearer, A., *Burgh Records of Dunfermline in the sixteenth and seventeenth centuries* Dunfermline (1951), 250. 'Sklaite' = A sloping surface, e.g. a slipway.

2. Houston, A.M., *Auchterderran, Fife: A Parish History* Paisley (1924), 424

3. Fife County Council, *Fife Looks Ahead* Edinburgh (1946), 11, 17

4. Thomson, J., *A General View of the Agriculture of the County of Fife* Edinburgh (1800), 291

5. Scott, Sir Walter, *Waverley Novels: The Fair Maid of Perth*, Vol. 1 Edinburgh (1903)★, 23: 'Childish wonder, indeed, was an ingredient in my delight . . . I recollect pulling up the reins without meaning to do so, and gazing on the scene before me as if I had been afraid it would shift like those in a theatre before I could distinctly observe its different parts'. The view was of Perth, from the old road, shown on Roy's map of 1755, from Burntisland or North Queensferry in Fife to Perth. An editorial note adds: 'The modern method of conducting the highways through the valleys and along the bases, instead of over the tops of mountains, as in the days when Chrystal Croftangry [Scott's hero] travelled, has deprived the stranger of two very striking points of view on the road from Edinburgh to Perth'. (The other view was from the hill of Moredun, or Moncrieff, on the north side of Strathearn.) ★ First published in 1814. Scott was born in 1771.

12

Road History on the Ground

For the more determined reader there follow field-notes that it is hoped will not only enhance interest in road history, but will form the basis for short excursions. The features mentioned are mostly accessible by public roads. Otherwise, wherever a patent right of way exists, this has been chosen.

In each section a starting place is in bold type and is, where possible, a vantage point also.

Since some effort will be required to acquire the principal maps (Ordnance Survey Sheets 58 and 59) and travel round Fife, there should be more detailed references than were appropriate in earlier chapters. Where works are readily identifiable from the author's name in the Bibliography the reference is simplified, e.g. Bennett (1983.7); for road authority records at Fife Region offices in Glenrothes the following abbreviations are used: C/Cu/D/K/S.S/T — i.e. County/Cupar/Dunfermline/Kirkcaldy/St Andrews. Statute Labour/Turnpike Trust. Thus 'C.S 17.3.1809' = the minutes of the county meeting of statute labour trustees of that date. The volume to ask for may be identified from the National Register of Archives for Scotland (NRAS) index, of which there is a copy in the Glenrothes file room, in St Andrews University Library and at Register House, Edinburgh.

Strathkinness Crossroads (459164) where the roads from Dundee to Elie/Largo and from St Andrews to Cupar intersect. One of the corner buildings to the north may have been a tollhouse between 1850, when its tolls were first rouped, and 1855, the year of the six-inch map on which it is shown. Unfortunately, the lettering is ambiguous as to its exact position. To the north note Guardbridge, repaired by Archbishop Beaton in 1592.[1] The modern replacement was started in 1936 (Fig. 12.1). The Minister of St Andrews parish recalls in 1793 that there 'was wont to be stretched an iron chain, which was opened only for chaises'; other vehicles were expected to wait for low tide and ford the Eden (O.S.A. 10, 733).

To the right, the Coble Shore (467195) provided a landing place for boats carrying goods for Cupar, and also a fording point opposite Cable House Point. Shelly Point (473200) was sufficiently popular as a landing place for Henderson of Earlshall to ask for the shore road to the

Fig. 12.1. The Old Guard Bridge, photographed in 1936, just before it was to be obscured by the modern structure. The parish minister recalled in 1793 that a chain was placed across the far end, removed only for chaises. Humbler vehicles had to wait for low tide to ford the Eden. Two buildings are seen which controlled traffic, both now demolished — the road toll-house (above the further abutment) and the railway signal box.

north to be closed (C.T 28.7.1818), for he claimed the traffic was cutting up the road.

Down Kincaple Loan on the left, the farm steading (460184) contains the walls of the original Haig distillery, shown by Ainslie (1775). Until the cutting near the farm was made, the loan would have been uncomfortably steep at this point, and the route to Guardbridge shown by Roy's map went down Kincaple Den where the footpath runs today (Fig. 2.3). The Guardbridge tollhouse was shifted more than once, but its final position can be seen in Figure 12.1. A valuable but elusive customer was Haig, who had switched his distillery to the site of the present papermill.[2] At high tide, coal, barley and other materials for making his cherished liquid could be landed at a quay and avoid passing the tollbar. Another source of irritation to the trustees was a convenient bypass route past Haig's house at Seggie on which a gate had to be fixed, with a key only for use on Sundays. His principal adversary was Cheape of Strathtyrum who called for a weighing

G

machine to check Haig's carts and questioned the adequacy of the compositions he paid for relief from tolls.

The location of Kincaple toll (Fig. 7.4) provoked a lengthy debate. The trustees were worried that to place it beyond Kincaple Loan to benefit from the six-mile rule 'would appear like artifice'. Nevertheless, there it stands. Kincaple Den was still usable, for the trustees saw it as a possible evasion route (C.T 25.8.1801), but what they did not foresee was that the tollkeeper himself could be persuaded, given the necessary monetary encouragement, to allow stone from Strathkinness to bypass the Argyll bar in St Andrews. The extra mileage was well worth the carter's while. Two roads run from Strathkinness to the west, the one via Bonfield, Easter Clatto and Blebo Craigs to Kemback, now disused; the other the old statute labour road to Cupar via Dairsie Bridge (Figs. 3.5 and 9.9). From the quarries at Nydie came most of the stone for the cathedral and town of St Andrews, and the waggon or sledge route to Balmerino Abbey leads down to a ford over the Eden, situated, according to R.F. Smith (1948), at 441184.

Bank South of Kilmany (387210). If approached from Cupar, note that the Bishopgait, shown as a through road by Ainslie, was closed by the owner of Pitfirrane (Cu.S 2.4.1806). The G.C.H.Q. installation at Hawklaw now stands on the old line. Take instead the North Burnside road and turn right to pick up the road to Kilmany. At 381178 is Street Ford, alongside the modern bridge. At the vantage point, note the zig-zag to ease the pull for the horses. This is the main route across the peninsula shown on Dorret's map of 1750 (Fig. 1.4), and remained in use up to 1800. Beyond Kilmany the road crosses the valley bottom to climb towards Gauldry, and past traffic has worn a deep hollow way up the opposite bank (387224). A section of the road, abandoned by modern farm traffic, is to be found in the trees between Shambleton Hill and Dandies Wood. Roy showed two roads diverging below this point, the one striking off to the right in the direction of Newton Hill, the other nearly reaching Gauldry before swinging east to rejoin the first (Fig. 12.2). Ainslie's road skirted Gauldry and went down through Peacehill and along the shore to Woodhaven.

Bank above Newton Farm (400244, Fig. 8.7). Early travellers to Woodhaven had to find their way through the hummocky post-glacial deposits which strew the valley bottom between here and Flass (411259), that is up to 1804, when Stewart of St Fort devised the present route through Wormit. The earlier road crossed the skyline above Flass, and was joined by another road from St Andrews which,

Fig. 12.2. The road through Cupar to Woodhaven. Passing through the village of Kilmany, the road (white dots) climbs the east shoulder of Round Hill, down into a hollow, and then through Dandies Wood over to Gauldry. It remained the principal route between Edinburgh and Dundee until after 1800. Roy's map of 1755 shows an alternative branch (line of dashes) over the ridge of Newton Hill. See also Fig. 8.7.

to the annoyance of the owner, carried cartloads of manure past the windows of St Fort. His answer was to build a road from the site of the present roundabout (419248) to connect with the new Wormit road. Before closure, the Flass bank road had been realigned on the north slope to avoid the steepest parts and is walkable down to near Woodhaven pier (Fig. 8.8).

A general view of both the routes north of Kilmany and of Flass Bank can be gained from **Lucklaw Hill** (419216), from which can also be seen the Cupar road to the bridge over the Motray Water at Brackmont Mill (440224), and the route taken by Berry of Tayfield to the rival ferry of Newport (Road 37).

Drumcarrow (460133). West of the junction at Denhead (466134), broken ground marks the site of old ironstone workings. With nearby coal and limestone from the quarry in the wood to the east (471132) there were the ingredients for iron smelting. From Denhead a road led across what is now Craigtoun Park to Lumbo Bridge (488148), continuing as the Canongate right into St Andrews. Another road set off, now in part submerged beneath Cameron reservoir, to Radernie and the south coast. To the north can be seen the first vantage point at Strathkinness, and an intervening east-west ridge carries the Bishop's Road (Fig. 9.7), the modern road, No. 80 of the 1829 Act, running this side of it past Claremont (460145).

To the west of Drumcarrow, beyond Ladeddie Farm, is the old coal road into Cupar (Fig. 3.6). Between Drumcarrow and Wilkieston (450121) were numerous small-scale coalpits. A tractor nearly disappeared into one recently and the underground workings were mapped by a team of geographers under an archaeologist.[3] Coal was supplied to the limekilns at Backfield of Ladeddie (440137). The quarry is overgrown, but the limestone can be seen in the walls of the steading, near Road 80. The walker may continue from Drumcarrow straight on past Ladeddie Farm to view the glacial lake floor, crossed by the Ceres Burn before it plunges into the spectacular Dura den near Blebo Hole. The low-lying ground round Pitscottie may account for the former route to Cupar from below North Callange over the old bridge (Figs. 3.3 and 3.4) and up the opposite bank to Ceres Muir. It was sufficiently important for a tollbar to be placed at Sodom (412127). From Callange Bridge a causeway had to be built to reroute the Cupar road through Pitscottie, thence through Wester Dura and Balass (Road 14). The right to tolls at a new tollbar at Pitscottie crossroads was rouped in 1817.

Ceres Folk Museum (400113) has a fine collection of road history objects which will not be listed here, save for mentioning a copy of Ainslie's map and a toll schedule from Hammer Toll on Road 16. Nearby is the famous seventeenth-century packhorse bridge, the low parapets, 6ft 6ins apart at the crown, allowing packs to overhang. On an estimate being submitted for its repair (Cu.S 22.5.1786), it was objected that it was not 'a Bridge for Wheel Carriages but only for passengers on foot and Horseback'. A ford upstream had been 'shut up and enclosed' by the landowner, but steps were to be taken to make the road 'patent' again. However, the modern bridge, built in 1881, now takes Road 48 over to Craigrothie.

From the green by the packhorse bridge the old ridge road to Struthers and Kennoway climbs away to the south-west. Like many such roads where the natural drainage along the ridge makes it passable at all seasons, it is known locally as the Waterless Road. The reader may care to walk to Road 13 at Struthers — a toll stood at the junction — or drive round via Craigrothie to the next vantage point.

Chance Inn Junction (377104). From here may be seen the course of the old Kennoway to Cupar road past Scotstarvit (Figs. 3.5 and 5.5). At the next junction to the north the two main lines of descent of Garley Bank (Figs. 3.5 and 3.2) show clearly, though the best overall view is from north of the Eden on Cupar Muir (Fig. 5.6). The continuation of the old Kennoway road to the south may be followed on foot, but a climb to the top of Hill of Tarvit is also rewarding. From the latter an interesting diversion at Crawford Priory can be seen at Clushford Toll (355114). The road formerly continued through what are now conifer plantations, the diversion taking place some time after 1828 (Sharp's map). The owner up to 1833 was easily offended and hired a band of policemen from Edinburgh to 'show . . . forth of the avenue' those who had incurred her displeasure.[4] In 1871 Lady Crawford's successor, the Earl of Glasgow, was reported as consenting to a diversion, paying the cost in return for possession of the solum (the ground occupied) of the older road.

From the Chance Inn junction one may travel by Road 13 to pick up the other end of the old road at Baintown (355037), pausing perhaps to consider why the road surveyor chose to give distances in sevenths of a mile on the milestones at 379099 and 382083.[5] The latter stop permits a short diversion to where the old road crosses at Muirhead, and a modest walk brings one to the steep-sided Clatto Den, possibly the principal reason for the major realignment proposed in the 1790 Act. In Kennoway itself, the main street has been diverted from its former narrow course and at Windygates another diversion can be seen, taking the modern road over both railway and river. Cameron Bridge is left in peace, on the site shown by Gordon in 1645. It has inherited from Guardbridge the company of a Haig distillery, this time upstream and close enough to encrust it with the pervasive black mould nourished by the vapours that seem to diffuse from whisky stores. A third bridge now carries the new Windygates bypass.

From Kennoway there are two statute labour roads over the hills to Road 10 from Cupar to New Inn, and a commanding view may be had from the coal and lime road **above Burnturk** at 336083. The River Eden winds across the broad Howe of Fife, an area in which the most radical changes in the eighteenth-century road pattern took place. Below us are two bridges, at Ramornie (329097) and Kingskettle (309090) which in Ainslie's time (1775) were connected by a maze of tracks picking their way through the gravelly mounds and intervening marshes of the Howe, to the rising ground beyond. A third bridge, at

Shiells (283086), gave access to Auchtermuchty by roads to the west of Rossie Loch, which was drained in the mid-eighteenth century, and to the east a road by Kinloch led to Newburgh and Perth.

A more direct route from Kennoway to the New Inn road lies through Langdyke (335047) and descends past the limestone workings at Forthar (302062) to which coal was brought through the New Inn tollbar, an imposition which coal owners like Balfour of Balbirnie were at pains to circumvent, even if it meant opening up a different coal route, such as that from Rameldrie, further east (Bennett 1983. 35-6).

The New Inn Junction (285052). From the low col between the East Lomond Hill and the hills towards the East Neuk, roads fan out across northern Fife. It was known up to the end of the eighteenth century as Pittillock Ford, from the burn crossing the Kirkcaldy road. The burn is peculiar in that it may now be seen from below where it is carried by an aqueduct over the railway cutting, after which it enters a former sub-glacial channel. The fall was used by Channelhall Mill (287062) as a source of power.

The present four-way junction dates from 1804. Before then the traveller from the south to Newburgh turned left and, after a few yards, north again through Freuchie and Shiels Bridge. The remains of this turnpike road (no. 12 of the 1790 Act) must now be approached from Freuchie. A broad grassy track now comes to an abrupt end in a cultivated field, but the six-inch sheet of 1855 shows it going right through to the Falkland road. Up to about 1983 there was even a bridge left stranded in the field by a diversion of the watercourse.

This part of Road 12 was made redundant by the building of the new bridge at Drumtenant (293086), from which the turnpike trustees were able to set out their splendid straight lines, a triumph of rationality over the previously chaotic roads of the Howe.

Before proceeding further we should take a closer look at the country to the north to which these new roads were directed.

Moonzie Kirk (338176). This may be approached from Cupar, bearing in mind that the late eighteenth-century road to Newburgh went past Springfield House (now Kinloss) and via Kilmaron to Muirside (349170), on to Parbroath, Ayton, Glenduckie along the northern slope of the valley, and over the east side of Lindores Hill. At Muirside a grass track diverges eastwards to Foodieash, Dairsie and Guardbridge.

From the Kirk we may survey the formerly waterlogged depressions gouged out by lobes of a Tay glacier. Leading past Dunbog and

Luthrie, they have now largely been drained and carry the modern roads of the 1797 Act. A depression to the east is still in its post-glacial state, providing a defensive marsh around Lordscairnie Castle (348178), and is crossed by the Foul Causeway near Myrecairnie, repaired in 1720. To the north-west is Luthrie, from which Robert Baillie, factor for his absent brother, organised much of the road system in the 1780s.

Letham (307144). To the east the track through Letham Farm leads towards Luthrie past Cantyhall, with a steep descent to Cunnoquhie Mill (Fig. 8.5). Several hill tracks towards Lindores and Newburgh start from the road between Cantyhall and Collessie, most interesting of which is the designated Road 17 of the 1790 Act (Fig. 5.7), drawn on John Ainslie's map of Scotland (1789). At Monimail a road from across the Howe formerly passed through the parks of Melville House and may be followed up the valley to the col at **Whitefield** (285158), where one may descend either to Dunbog or Lindores, the latter route crossing by a morainic ridge east of the loch. Note the incompletely drained hollow to the north of Parkneuk (277163), an example of what large areas of these depressions were like at the end of the eighteenth century. Between Monimail and Collessie is a curious case where a tenant — a weaver — has successfully resisted an attempt to move him. At Whinnypark (293138) the road has been obliged to make a neat detour round his cottage (Cu.S 2.4.1828).

At Collessie the presumed monks' road to Lindores Abbey (Fig. 8.2) passes through Braeside and east of Green Law (275147), a road repaired in 1734. At the crossroads, now staggered for road safety, was the Trafalgar Inn, appropriately named since the turnpike (No. 16) was completed in 1805. This was a frequent venue for meetings of the Cupar district trust. The road to this point from New Inn replaced one through the Kinloch estate, some of the tenants joining those who had been rehoused when the draining of Rossie Loch had changed their sources of employment. The old road took a hill route past Meadowells and Woodhead (263145), joining the Lumquhat road from Auchtermuchty south of Berryhill (258159). The new Road 34 of the 1797 Act had a tollbar called New York at 276139, which aroused local opposition. Pagan (1845.204) noted that it found itself one morning 'lying on its back, without a moving cause'.

Ormiston Hill (235175). From this point may be seen how the town of Newburgh was approached by roads past Old Parkhill (249183) and past Macduff's Cross (227167). The latter, No. 69 of the 1810 Act, was a non-starter with some hopelessly steep climbs. No. 67 through Pitcairlie was planned and worked on over many years, a tollhouse being erected at the junction with Road 69 before 1813. The stage coach 'Defiance' for some years took this route to Perth (K.T 30.5.1835 and Fig. 6.4).

Tollgates had been placed at both ends of Newburgh by 1801, the east bar at the junction with the Flisk road (241183) where a garage now stands, and the west bar at the junction with the Woodriffe road. It was the trade in timber, grain and flax passing through the port which prompted petitions in the 1770s from merchants in Auchtermuchty and Falkland for improved road access through the hills.

East Lomond Hill (244063). Many of the routes already described can be traced across the landscape from this point. Nearer at hand the focal position of the New Inn junction can be readily seen. The remains of the buildings behind the inn are among trees opposite the filling station. The tollbar was at the Kirkforthar junction (285045), roughly equidistant between the bars at Cupar and at Gallatown, and had the highest income in Fife. It was on the road to the south that Lord Rothes, with his coalpits at Cadham (277021), gained experience in road management in the 1740s. He, and Lord St Clair of Dysart, another coal owner, were the prime movers of road improvement after 1746.

At Balbirnie the road ran past the site of the present house along the north drive from Balfarg (286033). Balbirnie Bridge replaces a ford which remains beside it, and the Plasterers Inn was close to the River Leven to the south-east (Bennett 1983.10 and Bodie 1968.96). Downstream from here, on the north bank at 295010, were the Balgonie iron workings, from which heavy carts carried ore for shipment to the Carron foundry near Falkirk. The carts would cross Balgonie Bridge and reach the Kirkcaldy road through Coaltown of Balgonie. Balfour's response to complaints of excessive damage from his carts was to use a road from Sythrum (299009) to the port of West Wemyss, known locally as 'The Queen's Road', since Queen Mary is said to have used it to reach Falkland Palace.

South of the Balgonie junction some of the proposed termini for the central east-west road link may be identified. It is probable that the Plasterers Inn was never intended to be more than a recognisable landmark at the end of the road from Kirk of Beath (Road 8). When it came to considering the alternative routes in detail, the possible termini were Balfarg, Bankhead and a point '13 chains south of Bighty burn'. The latter corresponds closely to the line of a belt of woodland crossing the present dual carriageway at 285001 and continuing through to the older road to Cupar at Eastfield (Fig. 11.1).

At Thornton the road through Strathore was originally intended to bring coal from Ferguson of Raith's pits to Road 10, and its completion provided a partial solution to the problem of the east-west link, sufficient, that is, to postpone further action for one hundred and eighty years or so. In terms of a return on capital invested, Ferguson's enterprise was more successful than the more recent project of which the twin towers to the south of the road bear witness.[6] The Strathore road could have been continued in a straight line to Auchterderran and thence to the Kirk of Beath. The ultimate solution, the East Fife Regional Road, is scheduled to reach Redhouse (293953) before 1990.

Leslie and the Upper Leven. At Walkerton (233011) an ancient track has been honoured by the Ordnance Survey on their 1/25,000 Glenrothes sheet by printing the local names 'Bloodyfoot' and, north of the river, 'Strathendry Avenue', the latter meeting a 'Drove Road' which crosses the Lomonds. The section immediately south of the Leven is also marked 'Cadgergait' on the old six-inch map. It follows the side of a steep den and forms part of a network of tracks used for centuries by itinerant traders and carriers, most of whom would have carried their goods on one or more packhorses. To the west the Auchmuir Bridge is one of the earliest recorded bridges in Fife. Beyond it roads to Stirling and Perth diverge on either side of Loch Leven. The latter route is shown by Roy as starting from Burntisland and proceeding via Balmule, Auchtertool, Bow Bridge and Pitkinny, crossing the Gullet Bridge in Kinross before merging with the road from Auchmuir Bridge. From their it went through Balgedie, where cattle drovers are traditionally held to have been the principal customers, and re-entered Fife through Burnside, on the Cupar-Kinross road, leaving again over Paris Bridge (138114). From there, the traveller to Perth could take the Wicks of Baiglie road or the Wallace Road over the Ochils to Bridge of Earn (Fig. 11.2).

Burntisland and the West. Near Auchtertool, another road from Balmule crosses the Pilkham Hills to join the Great North Road at Cowdenbeath. Unfortunately, the section north of the ridge (191896) has been recently obliterated by the Mossmorran petrochemicals complex, but the section to the south at Drumpuddock (195894) that was excavated in the 1960s (Stephen 1975.243a) is still intact, if, as the

Fig. 12.3. The old Perth road from North Queensferry. This had been replaced before 1772 by the gentler sloping road to the left. The sign reads '20%' (or 1 in 5). A rather less steep descent to Jamestown toll is shown in Figure 5.2.

name suggests, somewhat waterlogged. As a means of reaching Perth, the M90 has distinct advantages.

Between Balmule and Aberdour a number of hillside routes have fallen into disuse, notably that from the entrance to Humbie on the coast road at 197859 to the junction opposite Dunearn (209871). East of Dalachy, at 210863, are the quarries from which Lord Morton had limestone carried in carts down to his harbour at Starleyburn (218859), the site of a tollbar (C.T 16.10.1806).

At 153842 the road to Inverkeithing crosses the waggonway from the Fordell coalpits to St David's harbour, a reminder that loads were drawn on rails, first of wood and then of iron, well before roads were brought up to a standard to carry the same traffic. A similar waggonway meets the Great North Road south of Bois Bridge (133836) and the old track bed can be followed up to the former collieries at Halbeath.

Jamestown Toll (127819) (Fig. 5.2). This renovated tollhouse provides a landmark in an otherwise bewildering pattern of rail and road alterations to the eighteenth-century scene. The replacement for Jamestown, known as North Ferry Toll, is now unrecognisable, but from Castlandhill (119827) one may work out the course of the graded route which replaced the steep climb up to the Crooks in 1776 (Fig. 5.3 and 12.3).

Along the shore to the west the massive limekilns of Lord Elgin's complex at Charlestown, with its railway bringing coal down from his pits west of Dunfermline, illustrate how a fortunate disposition of coal, limestone and a harbour could lead to a spectacular commercial success. From here burnt lime was exported to all parts of Scotland, and beyond.

A longer haul was required for the product loaded at Torryburn pier (015858) to which the railway came late. Ironstone was worked south of Comrie (020887), which had to be brought down three miles of winding track past Fernwoodlee (019877). The Forth Ironworks Company was set up in 1845 at Oakley (024892), where a school now stands, and before the extension of the railway to this point in 1850, additional coal had to be brought in by road, causing damage to the road from Dunfermline through Carnock (D.T 23.11.1846). The ironworks closed down in 1869, presumably after the ironstone had to be brought in from other locations.

Culross was not part of Fife until the boundary changes in 1889, but its earlier importance as a coalmining and manufacturing town had its inevitable influence on the development of roads to the east. Bruce's mine under the Forth is still evident in the remains of the platform, accessible at low tide, through which the coal was brought up, to be loaded directly onto vessels. The distress of King James VI in 1617 on emerging from the shaft is recorded by Cunningham (1910.91). The National Trust for Scotland owns many of the older buildings, which have been carefully restored, and Dunfermline District Council has also prepared a map of some of the early routes leading into the town. These include the Slate Loan, named after a seam of grey laminated sandstone running its full length, leading to the old town church, the West Kirk (980864). Both this and the Newgate (989860) to the Abbey will appeal only to the athletic and impermeably shod in their present condition. To the west of the West Kirk, the Moor Road formerly connected Culross to Kincardine, and joins the present A985 at 960870. By far the most popular feature is the street paving, the central strip of large flat stones, the 'croun o' the causey' having been a reserve of the privileged at a time when streets were used for dumping of refuse. They are now set flush with the adjacent cobbles to avoid damage to cars.

Fig. 12.4. The Croun o' the Causey, Culross. The Haggs or Stinking Wynd, one of several streets in which large flat stones were set along the mid-line. They were formerly raised above the adjoining cobbles to be clear of the refuse, and have been lowered for modern traffic.

Pittencrieff Park, Dunfermline. The Tower Bridge was the only means of access to the town from the west until the new bridge was built upstream in 1770. The tollhouse leased to David Brash in 1791 (p. 111) stood at the crossroads to the north-west of the park (083875). The waggon road from Lord Elgin's colliery at West Baldridge ran parallel to the road on the west side of Pittencrieff Park, leading to Charlestown lime works and harbour. One of the evasion routes of which Brash complained, the coal road to Berrylaw (082877 to 062878), is now a signposted footpath established by Dunfermline District Council planning department. Another, the road to Golfdrum, may be marked by the modern Golfdrum Road, which joins William Street at 082879.

NOTES

1. Inglis, H.R.G., 'The Roads and Bridges in the Early History of Scotland', *P.S.A.S.*, 47 (1913), 307

2. Weatherill, L., *A Hundred Years of Paper Making* Cupar (1974), Map 1

3. Proudfoot, E.V.W. (ed.), *Discovery and Excavation in Scotland* Scottish Group, Council for British Archaeology, Edinburgh (1979), 8

4. Connolly, M.F., *Eminent Men of Fife* Cupar (1866), 133

5. Stephen, W.M., 'Milestones and Wayside Markers in Fife', *P.S.A.S.*, 100 (1967-8). As Stephen records, the cast-iron plates were removed during the Second World War. In the early 1970s a St Andrews student conservation group, led by Professor J.F. Allen of the Physics Department, searched for and found a lost and buried milestone; following this, a team from the Department restored some seventy-five of the plates, by arrangement with the then Fife County Council. They were cleaned, repaired by welding where necessary, and repainted before refixing with stainless steel pins in lead plugs. One or two milestones, most of the wayside markers and most of the surviving Newport to Pettycur milestones still require attention. That in Figure 8.9 has been more fortunate. A survey of milestones and other road furniture has been carried out by the Scouts, the results of which may be seen in Ceres Folk Museum.

6. Ferguson, K., *A History of Glenrothes* Glenrothes (1982), 81

Bibliography

Abbreviations used in the Notes and Bibliography:

N.S.A.	New Statistical Account
O.S.A.	Old Statistical Account
P.S.A.S.	Proceedings of the Society of Antiquaries of Scotland
S.G.M.	Scottish Geographical Magazine
Trans.D.& G.N.H.A.S.	Transactions of the Dumfries and Galloway Natural History and Archaeological Society

Adam, W., *Letter to Rear-Admiral Adam M.P. from his father* Blairadam (1834)

Albert, W., *The Turnpike Road System in England 1663-1840* Cambridge (1962)

Allardyce, A. (ed.), *Scotland and Scotsmen in the Eighteenth Century* London (1888)

Anderson, A.D., 'The Development of the Road System in the Stewartry of Kirkcudbright 1590-1890', *Trans.D.& G.N.H.A.S.* 44 (1967) Pt 1 205-222, Pt 2 211-227

Appleton, J.H., *The Geography of Communications in Great Britain* London (1962)

Ash, M., 'Dairsie and Archbishop Spottiswoode', in *Scottish Church History Society Records* 21 Pt 2 (1976)

Bennett, G.P., *The Great Road between Forth and Tay* Markinch (1983)

Bird, A., *Roads and Vehicles* London (1969)

Bodie, W.G.R., 'Introduction to the Rothes Papers', *P.S.A.S.* 110 (1978-80), 403-431

Bodie, W.G.R., *Some Light on the Past around Glenrothes* St Andrews (1968)

Boswell, J: see Hill, G.B. (1964)

Brown, P.H. (ed.), *Early Travellers in Scotland* Edinburgh (1891)

Brown, P.H., *Scotland before 1700 from Contemporary Documents* Edinburgh (1893)

Bruce, W.S., *The Railways of Fife* Perth (1980)

Burghardt, A.F., 'The Origin and Development of the Road Network of the Niagara Peninsula of Ontario', *Annals of the Association of American Geographers* 59 (1969)

Burt, E., *Letters from a Gentleman in the North of Scotland* 2 vols. London (1815)

Chalmers, P., *Historical and Statistical Account of Dunfermline* Edinburgh (1844)

Coles, J.M., 'Prehistoric Roads and Trackways in Britain', in Fenton, A. and Stell, G. (eds.), *Loads and Roads in Scotland and Beyond* Edinburgh (1984)

Colville, J. (ed.), 'Letters of John Cockburn of Ormistoun to his gardener 1724-44', *Scottish History Society* 5 (1904)

Connolly, M.F., *Fifiana* Glasgow (1869)

Connolly, M.F., *Eminent Men of Fife* Cupar (1866)

Copeland, J., *Roads and their Traffic 1750-1850* Newton Abbot (1968)

Corbett, E., *An Old Coachman's Chatter* Wakefield (1974)

Cowan, W. and Boog Watson, C.B., *The Maps of Edinburgh 1544-1929* Edinburgh (1932)

Cunningham, A.S., *Culross, Past and Present* Leven (1910)

Curtis, G.R., 'Roads and Bridges in the Scottish Highlands: the route between

Dunkeld and Inverness, 1725-1925', *P.S.A.S.* 110 (1978-80), 475-496

Davidson, J.T., *The Road of the Bluidy Feet* Kirkcaldy (1942)

Dean, P. and C., *Passage of Time* North Queensferry (1981)

Dowden, J. (ed.) 'The Chartulary of Lindores', *Scottish History Society* 5 Edinburgh (1903), 175

Dyos, H.J. and Aldcroft, D.H., *British Transport* Leicester (1969)

Fenton, A. and Stell, G. (eds.) *Loads and Roads in Scotland and Beyond* Edinburgh (1984)

Ferguson, J., *The Law of Roads, Streets and Rights of Way in Scotland* Edinburgh (1904)

Ferguson, K., *A History of Glenrothes* Glenrothes (1982)

Fife County Council *Fife Looks Ahead* Edinburgh (1946)

Gardiner, L., *Stage-Coach to John O'Groats* London (1961)

Graham, A., 'Archaeology on a Great Post Road' *P.S.A.S.* 96 (1962)

Graham, A., 'Archaeological Notes on some Harbours in Eastern Scotland' *P.S.A.S.* 101 (1968-9)

Grant, I.R. and Withrington, D.J., eds. see *The Statistical Account of Scotland*

Grierson, Dr., *St Andrews* Cupar (1838)

Haldane, A.R.B., *New Ways through the Glens* London (1962)

Haldane, A.R.B., *Three Centuries of Scottish Posts* Edinburgh (1971)

Hill, G.B., (ed.), revised Powell, L.F., *Boswell's Life of Johnson* 5 Oxford (1964)

Houston, A.M., *Auchterderran, Fife: A Parish History* Paisley (1924)

Inglis, H.R.G. and Cowan, I., 'Maps of Early Edinburgh' *S.G.M.* 35 (1919)

Inglis, H.R.G., 'The Roads and Bridges in the Early History of Scotland' *P.S.A.S.* 47 (1913) 303-333

Jackman, W.T., *The Development of Transportation in Modern England* Cambridge (1916)

Lamont, J., *The Chronicle of Fife, Diary of John Lamont of Newton 1649-72* Edinburgh (1810)

Logue, K.J., *Popular Disturbances in Scotland, 1780-1815* Edinburgh (1979)

Lyon, C.J., *History of St Andrews* London (1843)

Margary, I.D., *Roman Roads in Britain* London (3rd edn. 1973)

McAdam, J.L., *Remarks on the Present System of Road Making* London (1822)

Mitchell, A. (ed.), 'Macfarlane's Geographical Collections Vol. 1' *Scottish History Society* 51 (1906)

Moir, D.G., 'The Roads of Scotland: 2: Statute Labour Roads' *S.G.M.* 73 (1), 73 (3) (1957)

Morer, T., 'A Short Account of Scotland, 1689', in Brown, P.H. (ed.) *Early Travellers in Scotland* Edinburgh (1891), 266-90

New Statistical Account (NSA): see *The Statistical Account of Fifeshire* London (1845)

Old Statistical Account (OSA): see *The Statistical Account of Scotland*

Pagan, W., *Road Reform* Edinburgh (1845)

Pawson, E., *Transport and Economy: The Turnpike Roads of Eighteenth Century Britain* London (1977)

Powell, L.F. see Hill, G.B., (1964)

Proudfoot, E.V.W. (ed.), *Discovery and Excavation in Scotland* Scottish Group, Council for British Archaeology, Edinburgh (1979)

Pryde, G.S. *The Burghs of Scotland: a critical list* London (1965)

Reader W.J., *Macadam: The McAdam family and the Turnpike Roads 1798-1861* London (1980)

Road Authority Records, Fife Regional Council, Glenrothes

Roberts, E., (ed.) *Louisa, Memories of a Quaker Childhood* London (1970)

Robertson, E.S., *Old St Andrews* London (1923)

Robertson, G., *Rural Recollections* Irvine (1829)

Rogers, C., *Rental Book of the Cistercian Abbey of Cupar-Angus* London (1879) 2 vols.

Royal Scottish Geographical Society, (Moir, D.G., ed.), *The Early Maps of Scotland to 1850 pt 2* Edinburgh (3rd edn. 1983)

Salmond, J.B., *Wade in Scotland* London (1938)

Sharp, J., 'Journey Chairgis from Edinburgh to St Androis', in Brown, P.H. (ed.) *Early Travellers in Scotland* Edinburgh (1891), 319-22

Shearer, A., *Burgh Records of Dunfermline in the sixteenth and seventeenth centuries* Dunfermline (1951)

Sibbald, R., *The History, Ancient and Modern, of the Sherrifdoms of Fife and Kinross . . . a new edition* Adamson, L. (ed.) Cupar (1803) (originally published 1710)

Silver, O.B., *The Development of the Fife Road System 1700-1850* Unpublished Ph.D. thesis University of St Andrews (1984)

Silver, O.B., 'The Roads of Scotland: from statute labour to tolls', *S.G.M.* (1987) (in press)

Sinclair, G.A., 'The Scottish Progress of James VI' *Scottish Historical Review* 10, (1913), 21-28

Skelton, R.A., 'The Military Survey of Scotland 1747-1755', *The Royal Scottish Geographical Society* Special Publication No. 1

Smiles, S., *Lives of the Engineers* (1904)

Smith, R.F., 'Quarry to Abbey: An Ancient Fife Route' *P.S.A.S.* 83 (1948-49) 162-7

Smith, S., *General View of the Agriculture of Galloway* London (1810)

Stephen, W.M., 'Milestones and Wayside Markers in Fife' *P.S.A.S.* 100 (1967-8), 179-184

Stephen, W.M., *The Industrial Archaeology of Fife 1790-1914* Unpublished Ph.D. thesis University of Strathclyde (1975)

Stephen, W.M., 'Toll-houses of the greater Fife area' *Industrial Archaeology* 4 (1967) 248-254

Taylor, C., *Roads and Tracks of Britain* London (1979)

Taylor, J., 'Description of the Parish of Monimail in Fife', in *Macfarlane's Geographical Collections* Mitchell, A. (ed.), Edinburgh (1906), 303-304

Taylor, W., *The Military Roads of Scotland* Newton Abbot (1976)

The Statistical Account of Fifeshire (contributed by The Ministers of the Respective Parishes) Edinburgh and London (1845) (referred to as the New Statistical Account or 'NSA')

The Statistical Account of Scotland 10 Grant, I.R. and Withrington, D.J. (eds.) Wakefield (1978) (referred to as the Old Statistical Account or 'OSA')

Thomson, J., *A General View of the Agriculture of the County of Fife* Edinburgh (1800)

Turnbull, W.H., *The Story of the Lomond Vale* Cupar (1911)

Weatherill, L., *A Hundred Years of Paper Making* Cupar (1974)

Webb, S. and B., *English Local Government: The Story of the King's Highway* London (1920)

Whetstone, A.E., *Scottish Country Government in the Eighteenth and Nineteenth Centuries* Edinburgh (1981)

Whittington, G. and Whyte, I.D., (eds.), *An Historical Geography of Scotland* London (1983)

Whittington, G., 'The Roy Map: The Protracted and Fair Copies – Part One' *S.G.M.* 102 (1986) 18-28 and 66-73

Whyte, I., *Agriculture and Society in Seventeenth Century Scotland* Edinburgh (1979)

Appendix
Roads in Fife designated as Turnpike Roads by Act of Parliament

---

1753 Act 26 GII 91 (See Fig. 5.1, page 58)

1 North Queensferry — Inverkeithing — (Kinross — Perth)
2 North Queensferry — Dunfermline — Torryburn — (Culross)
3 North Queensferry — Inverkeithing — Burntisland — Kirkcaldy

1790 Act 30 GIII 93 (See Fig 5.4, page 63)

4 Newmill Bridge — Foodies Mill — Inverkeithing — Aberdour — Kirkcaldy — Gallatown — Cameron Bridge — Crail
5 Newmill Bridge — Dunfermline — Crossgates — Auchtertool — Kirkcaldy
6 (Branch) — Crossford — Keavil — Ladysmill — Charlestown — Limekilns
7 Dunfermline — (westward) — (Perthshire)
8 The Plasterers — Kinglassie — Auchterderran — Kirk of Beath
9 Kirkcaldy — (northward) — / junction with Road 8
10 Kirkcaldy — New Inn — Cupar — Pitcullo — Dundee Waterside
11 New Inn — Falkland — Strathmiglo — (northward) — (Perthshire)
12 (Branch) — Shiels Bridge — Newburgh
13 Cupar — Kamesford — Letham — Kennoway — Cameron Bridge — / junction with Road 4
14 Cupar — Callange Bridge — Balcarres — / junction with Road 4
15 (Branch) — Lathockar Bridge — Crail
16 Cupar — Strathmiglo — (westward) — (Kinross-shire)
17 (Branch) — Letham — Newburgh — (Perthshire)
18 St Andrews — Guardbridge — / junction with Road 10 at Dronsmuir
19 Dundee Waterside — Guardbridge — Denhead — / junction with Road 14 at Radernie ground
20 Kirkcaldy — Dysart — (eastward) — / junction with Road 4

1797 Act 37 GIII 180 (See Fig. 5.8, page 70)

21 Road 4/ — Little Couston — Balmule — Kilrie — Kirkcaldy
22 Windygates Toll Bar — Balfarg
23 (Branch) — Plasterers
24 Damhead (Glenfarg) — / junction with Road 9
25 (Branch) — Damhead — Strathmiglo
26 The Dundee Ferries — (Kinross-shire)[1]
27 (Branch) — Balmerino Parish — Flisk — Newburgh

28 (Branch) — Balmerino Parish — Kilmany Parish — Cupar
29 (Branch) — Creich Parish — Moonzie Parish — Cupar
30 (Branch) — Abdie Parish — Denbog Parish — Newburgh
31 (Branch) — Monimail Parish — Cupar
32 (Branch) — Collessie Parish — Kettle Parish — New Inn
33 Balmalcolm — Falkland
34 Newburgh — Kinloch — Shiels Bridge — / junction with Road 11
35 Falkland — Kennoway
36 Road 13/ — Letham Mill Burn Bridge — Leven
37 Brackmontmill — Newport

[1] The terminus of Road 26 is given as Shiels Bridge in s.9 of the 1829 Act

1802 Act 42 GIII 97 (See Fig. 5.10, page 73)

38 (Causewayhead near Stirling — Dollar) — West Saline — Crossford — / junction with Road 4

1805 Act 45 GIII 108

39 Dunfermline — Balmule — Gask — Nivingston — / junction with Alloa Turnpike Road west of Tullibole
40 The High Road near Saline/ — (eastward) — Roscobie — The Stone Road — / junction with Road 1 south of Kelty

1807 Act 45 GIII 11

41 Brackmontmill — Ferryport
42 St Andrews — Kingsbarns — Crail
43 St Andrews — Lathones — / junction with Road 14 at Largoward
44 (Branch) — Higham Loan
45 St Andrews — Dunino — Anstruther Harbour
46 (Branch) — Nether Carnbee — Pittenweem Harbour
47 St Andrews — Balone — / junction with Road 19
48 St Andrews — Magus Muir — Ceres — / junction with Road 13
49 Cupar — Teasses — Largo Burn Mouth
50 Balcarres Mill — Kilconquhar — Elie Harbour
51 Road 4 at Balchrystie / — Elie — Pittenweem
52 Road 14 / — Fawfield — Pratis Muir — / junction with Road 13
53 Road 4 / — Kellie — Balhouffie — / junction with Road 45 at Pitkierie
54 (Branch) — Back of Balhouffie — Crail
55 Road 10 at Thornton / — Strathore — Cluny — / junction with Road 8
56 Callange — Pitscottie Bridge — Dura Den or Rumgay Ford — / proposed road Osnaburg — Ceres Muir
57 Road 4 at foot of Boreland Loan / — East Wemyss — Mooredge — Sawmill Ford — / junction with Road 4 at Scoonie Bridge

1809 Act 50 GIII 31 (see also 1 and 2 GIV 28 of 1821)

58 'The New Line of Road' (or Road 1 at Cowdenend — Road 1 at Blairadam Bridge)

1810 Act 50 GIII 72

59 Road 40 / — Pitcairn Mill — / junction with Road 8
60 Road 39 / — Burt's Coal Hill — Lochend — Red Craigs — Outh — Hillside — (Powmill — Yetts, in Perthshire)
61 Road 5 at Town Green / — Bellyeoman — Kingseat — North Meikle Beath — / junction with Road 1 at Kirk of Beath
62 (Branch) — Lassodie Mill — (across old section of road 1) — / junction with Road 58 north of Netherton
63 Road 58 / — White Rashes Road — Burntisland Harbour
64 Road 38 at Bambo Bridge / — (lands of Carnock, Comrie, West Grange, Brucefield) — / Road Kincardine — Alloa at Kennet
65 road 38 near West Luscar / — Clune — Drumtuthill — Coaltown — Lochend — / junction with Road 29 at Meldrumsmiln
66 (Branch) — Craigluscar — Myrie Hall — / junction with Road 40
67 Auchtermuchty — Moniefred — Lumquhat Miln — Pitcairlie — Denmill — Newburgh
68 (Branch at Pitcairlie) — Weddersbrae Den — / junction with Road 16 near Rossie
69 (Branch at Pitcairlie) — Macduff's Cross — / junction with Road 34
70 Leslie — (Scotlandwell in Kinross-shire)
71 (Branch across Gullet Bridge — east of Kirkness) — Kinglassie
72 Leslie — Balbedie — (Kirkness — the Brackleys) — Shanks of Navity — (The Binn and Barns — Nivingston in Kinross-shire)

1829 Act 10 GIV 84 (See Fig. 5.12, page 77)

73 Road 14 at Loans Toll Bar / — Kirkton of Largo
74 Road 16 near Gateside / — (Perthshire section of Road 1 at Beansnook)
75 Falkland — Dunshelt — Auchtermuchty
76 Road 9 at Bennochy / Sauchanbush — Torbain — Shawsmill / Road Lochgelly — Kirk of Beath
77 (Branch, across south-east part of Wester Bogie) — Chapel — / junction with Road 9
78 West Bridge of Innertiel — (northward) — Abbotshall Gate / Road 5
79 Leslie — Cabbagehall Bridge — (southward) — Inchdairney / Road 9
80 St Andrews — Balone — Claremont — Magask — Laleddy / Road 48 at Blebohole
81 Dunfermline — Pitbauchlie — Duloch — Fordell — Balbougie — Hillend
82 Whitehill Toll Bar — Aberdour Harbour
83 Ferryport — Spearhill — Newport
84 Dunfermline — (farms of Grange, Gellets, Blackhall, Primrose, Rosyth, Orchardhead) — North Queensferry
85 (Branch, through Rosyth Farm) — / junction with Road 4
86 Road 4 / — (through Abden grounds) — Pettycur

1839 Act 2 and 3 Vict. 48

87 Road 57 to be diverted at eastern end from Sawmill Ford to Proposed new bridge at Leven

1842 Act 5 and 6 Vict. 51

88 New Burntisland Pier — Kinghorn

Index